Public Policy and Politics

Series Editors: Colin Fudge and

Important shifts in the nature of public policy making are taking place, particularly at the local level. Increasing financial pressures on local government, the struggle to maintain public services, the emergence of new areas of concern, such as employment and economic development, and increasing partisanship in local politics, are all creating new strains but at the same time opening up new possibilities.

The series is designed to provide up-to-date, comprehensive and authoritative analysis of public policy and politics in practice. Public policy involves the expressing of explicit or implicit intentions by government which result in specific consequences for different groups within society. It is used by power-holders to control, regulate, influence or change our lives and therefore has to be located within a political context. Two key themes are stressed throughout the series. First, the books link discussion of the substance of policy to the politics of the policy-making process. Second, each volume aims to bridge theory and practice. The books capture the dynamics of public-policy-making but, equally important, aim to increase understanding of practice by locating these discussions within differing theoretical perspectives. Given the complexity of the processes and the issues involved, there is a strong emphasis on interdisciplinary approaches.

The series is focused on public policy and politics in contemporary Britain. It embraces not only local and central government activity, but also central–local relations, public-sector/private-sector relations and the role of non-governmental agencies. Comparisons with other advanced societies will form an integral part of appropriate volumes. Each book presents and evaluates practice by drawing on relevant theories and applying them to both the *substance* of policy (for example, housing, employment, local government finance) and to the *process* of policy development and implementation (for example, planning, management, organisational and political bargaining).

Every effort has been made to make the books in the series as readable and usable as possible. Our hope is that it will be of value to all those interested in public policy and politics – whether as students, practitioners or academics. We shall be satisfied if the series helps in a modest way to improve understanding and debate about public policy and politics in the 1990s.

Public Policy and Politics
Series Editors: Colin Fudge and Robin Hambleton

PUBLISHED

Kate Ascher, *The Politics of Privatisation*
Gideon Ben-Tovim, John Gabriel, Ian Law and Kathleen Stredder, *The Local Politics of Race*
Christopher C. Hood, *The Tools of Government*
Martin Laffin, *Managing under Pressure: Industrial Relations in Local Government*
Peter Malpass and Alan Murie, *Housing Policy and Practice* (3rd edition)
K. Newton and T.J. Karran, *The Politics of Local Expenditure*
Gerry Stoker, *The Politics of Local Government*
Ken Young and Charlie Mason (eds), *Urban Economic Development*

FORTHCOMING

Jacqueline Barron, Gerald Crawley and Tony Wood: *The Private Face of Politics*
Danny Burns, Robin Hambleton and Paul Hoggett, *The Politics of Decentralisation*
Tony Eddison and Eugene Ring, *Management and Human Behaviour*
Aiam Eisenschitz and Jamie Gough, *Local Economic Initiatives*
Robin Hambleton, *An Introduction to Local Policy-Making*
Clive Harris, Michael Keith and John Solomos, *Racial Inequality and Public Policy*
Patsy Healey, *Places We Could Make: The Future of Environmental Planning*
Ian Henry, *The Politics of Leisure Policy*
Stewart Lansley, Sue Gossh and Christian Wolmar, *Councils in Conflict: The Rise and Fall of the Municipal Left*

The Tools of Government

Christopher C. Hood

M
MACMILLAN

First edition 1983
Reprinted 1990

Published by
MACMILLAN EDUCATION LTD
Houndmills, Basingstoke, Hampshire RG21 2XS
and London
Companies and representatives
throughout the world

Printed in Hong Kong

ISBN 0–333–34396–4

Contents

Acknowledgements

For a short book, this has been a longish time in the making, and I have many debts to acknowledge.

I suppose that there are three ideal conditions for writing a book: the opportunity to work out one's ideas periodically with others who are 'on the same wavelength'; a place to write which combines mental stimulation with relative freedom from day-to-day pressures; and an understanding and enthusiastic publisher. Lots of books – and good ones, too – somehow get written without some, or even any, of these conditions. But for this book I was lucky enough to enjoy all three.

When it came to discussing ideas, I am chiefly indebted to Andrew Dunsire, with whom I first began to think seriously about this subject when I worked at the University of York from 1977 to 1979. He was also of great help subsequently, and he read an earlier draft of this book, making valuable suggestions for improvement and allowing me to incorporate them. If the finished product does not meet his exacting standards, the fault is certainly mine, not his.

I have also benefited from comments offered by many others, including Richard Rose, Charles Raab and Bill Mackenzie (whose comments on my first paper on this subject – quite rightly – induced me to tear it up and try again). Thoughts about and sections of this book have been presented at seminars at the universities of Manchester, Durham, Edinburgh and Bielefeld, and I have profited greatly from the critical (sometimes very critical!) reactions to those presentations.

For the provision of a place to write, I am eternally grateful to the incomparable 'ZiF' (Zentrum für interdisziplinäre Forschung at the University of Bielefeld). ZiF supplied an ideal environment for producing the last two drafts of this book in the spring and summer of 1982 when, at the invitation of Franz-Xaver Kaufmann, I took part in a multidisciplinary seminar programme on 'Steuerung und Erfolgskontrolle im öffentlichen Sektor' (guidance, control and performance evaluation in the public sector). This broadened my horizons – intellectually, geographically and even linguistically – and released me from that iron (Gresham's) law of university teaching: that day-to-day trivialities drive out reflection and innovation. I am deeply grateful to Franz Kaufmann and also to the many stimulating colleagues whom I encountered at ZiF, in particular Lin and Vincent Ostrom, Nino Majone, Paul Sabatier and Jim Sharpe.

The third part of the recipe is the publisher. I have been very encouraged by the enthusiasm and active interest taken in this book by Steven Kennedy of Macmillan, and I am also grateful for guidance and criticism from the series editors, Colin Fudge and Robin Hambleton. All three offered constructive ideas for improving an earlier draft of the book.

Finally, I am deeply grateful to my wife, who has lived with this for a long time, and has cheerfully helped with editing, proofing, tracking down references and eliminating some of the grosser infelicities of style. She also compiled the index.

CHRISTOPHER HOOD

List of Tables and Figures

Tables

Figures

Guide to Reading the Book

First, be warned. This book will *not* tell you everything you ever wanted to know about government. The quick imaginations of political and other scientists have contrived any number of ways in which 'government' can be explored and understood, and this book does not even try to catalogue, let alone synthesise, those approaches. It is a deliberately one-eyed approach to its subject.

What the book *does* aim to do is to help you to look at 'government' in one rather particular and unfamiliar way – as a set of basic tools or instruments which have to be continually drawn upon, combined in varying mixes and applied to the staggering multiplicity of tasks which modern government is (or feels) called upon to undertake. Many discussions of government activity include vague references to, or instances of, government's 'instruments', but very rarely is any attempt made to lay these out as a group for the layperson to see. That is what this book aims to do. It has been kept as brief and simple as possible, with the needs of the general reader and the student in mind rather than those of the emeritus professor.

Of course, everyone knows that you cannot really lay out government's tools in exactly the same way that a joiner or a plumber could do with the instruments he uses. Government's 'tools' are not directly observable. To 'see' them requires interpretation, and the spectacles needed are those of administrative analysis. The interpretation offered here is necessarily a personal one, though it has some resemblance to those produced by others. Certainly it is not to be taken as the last word on the subject.

Every book has chapters which can be skipped at a pinch. Don't skip Chapter 1. It is the key to the book. It sketches out the basic elements of government's tool-kit, related to government's resources and functions, and this needs to be read carefully in order to understand what follows. Some jargon is inescapable in a book like this. Substitute your own if you like, if it helps. The names used are only labels.

After that, the book could in principle be read in any order. It is laid out in the way that it is because it assumes that most readers will not be familiar with the operation of government in any detail, and will therefore want to see the simple framework of Chapter 1 fleshed out and discussed (which is what happens in Parts I and II) before going on to different questions. On the other hand, if you are really impatient to get to the 'payoff line', you may want to move straight to the chapters in Part III which set out some of the applications and implications which can be derived from looking at government activities through the lenses used here. At the beginning of each Part, you will find a short introduction explaining the framework of that set of chapters.

1 Exploring Government's Toolshed

To ask 'What does government do?' is to state a plain man's question in plain man's language. The answer is by no means simple.

(Rose, 1976, p. 247; and Rose and Peters, 1978, p. 67)

Well, what *does* government do, exactly?

Responding to this 'plain man's question' isn't simple, because there are so many possible ways in which it could be answered. Consider only three, out of a myriad of possibilities.

One possible reply would be to try to describe what happens 'inside' government. How decisions are made, how orders are passed down the line, how information moves about. If we chose to answer the question in this way, we would be telling a story about government's decision processes. It is the kind of story that has become familiar through political diaries and memoirs. The story would be punctuated by telephone calls and documents, interminable meetings, lights burning into the night, petty squabbles and jealousies, panics, heart attacks and nervous breakdowns, actors of varying importance, competence and ambition. We would soon become immersed in all those interesting but elusive questions about power, influence, who-said-what-to-whom and when. Not 'plain man's' territory, exactly.

But that is only one way of looking at what government does. A second type of answer might focus on the *subjects* in which governments today are interested, rather than on the arcane plottings in the chancelleries. That would take us on to an entirely different tack. We would find ourselves trying to list everything that government nowadays concerns itself with, for one reason or another. Very quickly that list would become bewilderingly long and heterogeneous. From government's birth control pills for cats in Denmark to its seals on domestic gas meters in Britain: government's spoor (its cloven hoof, some would say) appears everywhere. We would soon have to simplify, reducing the mass of specific interests down to a few major and general purposes that governments have, or say they have.

Either of these approaches would make sense as a way of describing 'what government does'. A third possibility – different again – is to describe the *tools* that government uses, rather than what it uses those tools for or how it reaches its decisions. We can imagine government as a set of administrative tools – such as tools for carpentry or gardening, or anything else you like. Government administration is about social control, not carpentry or gardening. But there is a tool-kit for that, just like anything else. What government does to *us* – its subjects or citizens – is to try to shape our lives by applying a set of administrative tools, in many different combinations and contexts, to suit a variety of purposes.

These three approaches to 'what governmnent does' are rather like the story of the blind men describing an elephant: each gets part of the whole picture. This book however is about 'what government does' only in the third sense. It is about the tools or instruments that government uses at the point where it comes into contact with 'us', the world outside. It focuses on the mechanics rather than on the ends of government, and on what government does to society rather than on what happens inside government.

This chapter briefly sets the scene, in four sections. The first section lays out some of the different kinds of basic tools which government has available to it. The aim is to provide the reader with an outline plan of government's tool-shed which will be explored further in later chapters. The second section is an explanation of what can be got out of looking at government from a 'tool-kit' perspective; in other words, why it is worth reading the book. The third section is an explanation of the focus and limitations of the approach being taken here, in the hope of avoiding confusion as to what the book is about. The fourth is a 'road map' – a brief explanation of the structure of the book.

Government as a tool-kit

If we were looking at a physical collection of tools, we could 'take in' that collection more easily if we could separate its contents into a few broad types at the outset, distinguishing (say) hammering tools from digging tools, measuring tools and cutting tools. When it comes to government's collection of tools – which are not physically assembled in a single place – it is all the more important to be able to identify broad classes if we are to avoid being swamped by detail and unable to distinguish theme from variations. By making two sets of simple distinctions, we can begin to make sense of the apparent complexity of the instruments which government uses on us.

Detectors and effectors

First, we can distinguish between government's tools for 'dectection' and its tools for 'effecting'. These are shown in Figure 1.1. *Detectors* are all the instruments that government uses for taking in information. *Effectors* are all the tools that government can use to try to make an impact on the world outside.

The terms 'detector' and 'effector' will be strange to some readers. They come from cybernetics, the science of general control systems (see Dunsire, 1978, pp. 59–60). They are the two essential capabilities that any system of control must possess at the point where it comes into contact with the world outside. This applies literally to *any* control

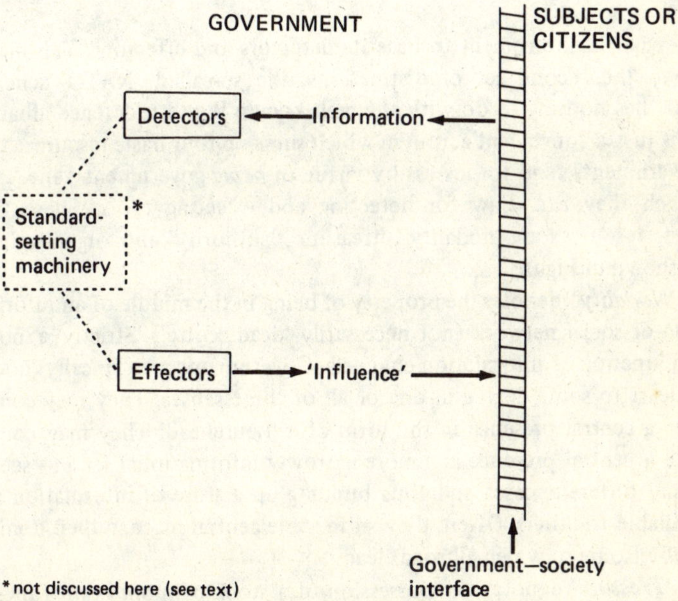

FIGURE 1.1 Government detectors and effectors

system in art or nature (a mousetrap, a moon rocket, the body's temperature control). For government, which is – or aims to be – pre-eminently a way of controlling society, these capabilities are basic to its existence.

Plainly, then, government needs to employ a host of detecting instruments to observe or to obtain information from the outside world. It is essential for any control system to have some means of ascertaining the state of the system or of the world outside as it relates to that control system – temperature, pressure, or whatever it may be.

But it is not enough simply to know what is going on. No control system is worthy of the name unless it is capable of taking some *action* on the basis of that knowledge. This is the second point at which any control system comes into contact with the world outside. It must have some means of trying to adjust the state of the system to which it relates. Here we come to the 'business end' of government – a range of tools which vary from the gentlest of blandishments to extremely blunt instruments.

The 'NATO' scheme – government's basic resources

On what is government to base its detectors and effectors? This brings us to the second set of distinctions, the so-called 'NATO' scheme. This has nothing to do with the well known Western defence alliance. It is just a convenient acronym which sums up four basic resources that governments tend to possess by virtue of *being* governments, and upon which they can draw for detecting and effecting tools. These four basic resources are 'nodality', 'treasure', 'authority' and 'organisation', as shown in Figure 1.2.

'*Nodality*' denotes the property of being in the middle of an information or social network (not necessarily 'dead centre'). Strictly, a 'node' is a junction of information channels. Governments are typically 'nodal' at least to some degree in one or all of three senses. They may constitute a central presence in the form of a 'figurehead' They may constitute a central presence in a more narrowly informational sense – seeing many different cases and thus building up a store of information not available to others. Often, they sit in some central place in their domain – the Rome to which all roads lead.

'*Treasure*' denotes the possession of a stock of moneys or 'fungible chattels'. That means not only (or necessarily) money in the common,

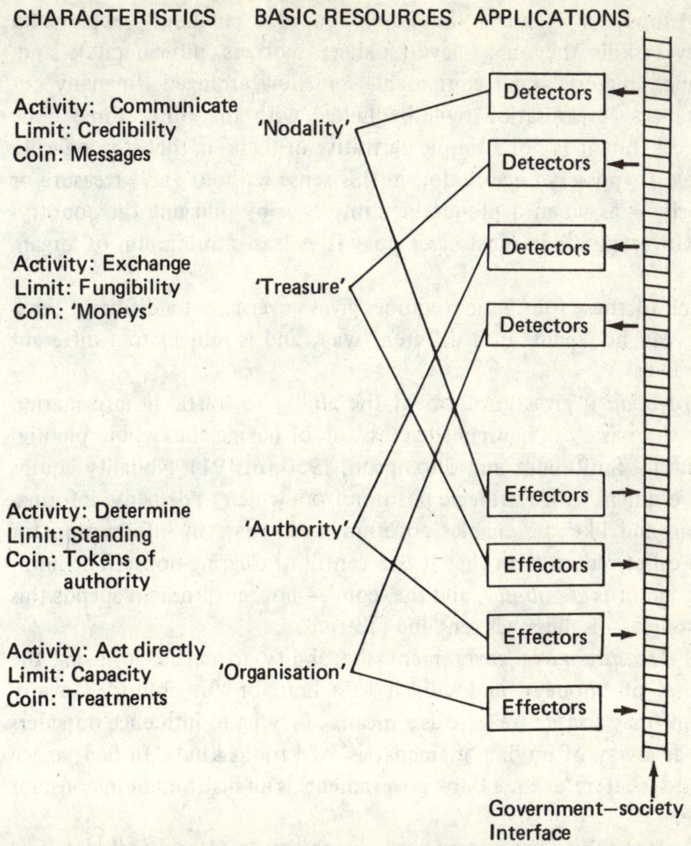

FIGURE 1.2 Eight basic types of government tool

everyday sense of banknotes or coins, but anything which has the money-like property of 'fungibility' (Rose and Peters, 1978, p. 25) – that is, the capacity to be freely exchanged. Governments in most cases possess at least some stock of 'treasure' in this sense.

'*Authority*' denotes the possession of legal or official power (Lasswell and Kaplan, 1950, p. 76, n. 2). That is the power officially to demand, forbid, guarantee, adjudicate. 'Authority' in this sense is traditionally seen as one of the defining properties of government, though its source, base and level may vary widely.

'*Organisation*' denotes the possession of a stock of people with whatever skills they may have (soldiers, workers, bureaucrats), land, buildings, materials and equipment, somehow arranged. In many circumstances 'organisation' will be linked with the other three basic resources, but it is not a simple derivative of them, in that it is logically possible to possess organisation in this sense without (say) treasure or authority – as when a plundering army lives by pillaging the countryside. Governments in most cases possess at least a minimum of 'organisation'.

Each of these four basic resources gives government a different capability, can be 'spent' in a different way, and is subject to a different limit. Thus:

(1) *Nodality* gives government the ability to traffic in information on the basis of 'figureheadedness' or of having the 'whole picture' (Simon, Smithburg and Thompson, 1950, p. 191). Nodality equips government with a strategic position from which to dispense information, and likewise enables government to draw in information for no other reason than that it *is* a centre or clearing-house. The limiting factor is *credibility*, and the 'coin' – how government spends this resource – is messages sent and received.

(2) *Treasure* gives government the ability to exchange, using the 'coin' of 'moneys' and subject to a limit of 'fungibility'. Government may use its treasure as a means of trying to influence outsiders or as a way of buying 'mercenaries' of various kinds. In fact, as we will see later, 'cheque-book government' is an instrument in constant use.

(3) *Authority* gives government the ability to 'determine' in a legal or official sense, using tokens of official authority as the coin, and subject to a limit of legal *standing*.

(4) *Organisation* gives government the physical ability to act directly, using its own forces rather than mercenaries. The coin is 'treatments' or physical processing, and the limiting factor is *capacity*.

As can be seen from Figure 1.2, each of these four properties can be used as the basis for tools both of detecting and effecting. Thus government can obtain information simply on account of its nodality (or by making itself nodal), by buying it, by officially demanding it, or by extracting it by means of some physical device. Similarly it can try to influence the world outside by sending out messages on the basis of its nodality, by treasure, by authority and by organisation.

These four resources are different in several ways, as I will indicate in later chapters. For example, some may be 'self-renewing', while others cannot be. And some may introduce more constraint into the environment of government's subjects than others. Very roughly, that level of constraint could be said to rise as government moves from nodality-based tools to those based on treasure, and then to authority-based and in turn to organisation-based tools. In very simple terms it could be said that 'nodality' works on your knowledge and attitudes, 'treasure' on your bank balance, 'authority' on your rights, status and duties, and 'organisation' on your physical environment or even on your person.

By combining the two control mechanisms and the four types of resources – as in Figure 1.2 – we get eight basic kinds of tool that government can use at the point were it comes into contact with the world outside. Each of these eight types will be discussed and explored further in subsequent chapters.

Pay-offs of the 'tool-kit perspective'

This book is by no means the first or only attempt to explore the tools used by government. Interested readers may want to compare the approach taken here with those of other authors (see the 'Guide to Further Reading' at the end of the book). There are any number of alternative ways of laying out government's tools, no one of which is necessarily 'right'. We could refine or sub-divide *ad infinitum*, depending on whether we want a scale that is large or small, general or area-specific.

But here we will not compare minor differences of classification as between one author and another. This is not that kind of book. A question that *does* need to be pursued, however, relates to the 'pay-offs' derivable from the 'tool-kit' approach to government. What advantage could there be in looking at government in this way, as opposed to our other two possible ways of describing what government does – a 'decision-making' or 'field of activity' perspective? Three main kinds of 'pay-offs' are briefly discussed below.

Making sense of complexity

First, having a sense of the basic tools available to government helps us to make sense of what seems at first sight to be the bewildering complexity of modern government's operations. Look at goverment activities in terms of government's many purposes or interests, as we saw earlier, and the list is endless. Look at those activities as the application of a relatively small set of basic tools, endlessly repeated in varying mixes, emphases and contexts, and the picture immediately becomes far easier to understand.

In fact (to take an analogy to which we will return later) it is like approaching each object that we encounter as some combination of a relatively small number of chemical elements rather than as a completely new physical substance. By looking at things this way, we can easily understand something that we have not seen before and even invent hypothetical new combinations for ourselves.

Similarly, comparisons become much easier to handle; indeed, much of the fascination of exploring government's tools is to compare the instruments brought to bear on a certain problem by different governments or by the same government at different times. The same instrument may be used for many different purposes.

This is just as well, for if government really had to design a completely new tool for each new subject in which it became interested, it would require far greater powers of innovativeness and imagination than governments can in practice be expected to possess. As it is the same basic set of tools appears again and again as governments face up to 'new' problems, such as computer privacy, glue-sniffing, microlight aircraft and hang-gliders. Only the mixture varies. This means that if we can grasp the basics of government's tool-kit, we can have a better sense of what 'they' – government, officialdom, authority – can do in any given case and what problems they may face.

Picking the tool for the job

Thus – and this is the second main 'pay-off' – a knowledge of government's tool-set may be useful, not merely as a way of understanding government, but also for diagnostic purposes.

Government, like man himself, is a tool-using animal. If it desires (say) defence, education, health – even birth control for cats – it must find and employ instruments that will actually produce such things. Otherwise its 'policies' or purposes will be no more than fantasies. It is by applying its tools that government makes the link between wish and fulfillment.

It hardly needs to be said that this link is frequently problematic and highly politicised. Selecting the right tool for the job often turns out to be a matter of faith and politics rather than of certainty. Indeed, it is not uncommon to find that the choice of 'instruments' attracts much hotter political debate than the ends being sought. For example, aims like preventing suicide or anti-social drinking may seem unexceptionable, but how can they actually be attained? Will an extension of suicide-prevention counselling discourage suicide attempts or positively encourage people to flirt with death? Will an extension of the permitted opening hours for bars reduce or increase the incidence of anti-social drinking?

If the operation of government's tools were unproblematic, it could be left to 'technocrats', and the rest of us could concentrate on the purposes that government should pursue. Things are not like that in reality. Knowing something about what is in government's tool-kit can at least help us to think about ways of doing better when – as so often happens – things go wrong. Such knowledge enables us to survey the main kinds of implements that might be used to address any given subject with which government may find itself dealing. If one tool fails to answer the purpose in any particular case, we can look systematically for others which might do the job. Thinking in these terms can provide some antidote to the all-too-common assumption in government affairs that things could not possibly be handled in any other way than they are at present.

Picking the 'tools for the times'

The two 'pay-offs' discussed so far could apply at any time. But it could be argued that it is especially useful to look at government's tool-kit *now*. Three trends observable at the present time may tend to throw the focus on to government's instruments rather more than in the past.

The first might be called the pressures of 'mature social interventionism' by government. Over the past century or so government has expanded its concerns by beginning to act in many spheres in which it has not previously been active. Health, welfare, education – the story of modern government's expansion has been told many times before (see, for example, Rose, 1976; Rose and Peters, 1978; Fry, 1979).

What happens now? There are at least two possibilities: that the 'interventionist' objectives of the past are abandoned, at least to some degree (Rose and Peters, 1978; Wildavsky, 1980) or, in the words of Mishan (in Wilson and Skinner, 1976, p. 291) that 'the public will... continue to demand increased government surveillance, monitoring, control and protection'. If it is the latter, and the *purposes* of government interventionism are not to come into question, the emphasis may fall on re-thinking the *tools* for the job. A phase of colonising new policy areas by government might be succeeded by a phase of trying out alternative second- and third-generation instruments in policy areas which have already been occupied by government for some time.

A second trend which may serve to make the selection of government's tools more problematic than in the past is closely related to the first. This is the world-wide 'fiscal crisis of the state' (O'Connor, 1973). This fiscal crisis is the check on the growth of government revenue and spending on the scale which has been seen in many countries in recent decades, resulting in attempted government cutbacks and financial stringency of a kind which has become commonplace almost everywhere.

This too has the effect of directing attention to the search for 'new' government instruments – or maybe old instruments in a new context – for 'government on the cheap'. Governments seek to achieve results similar, to, or better than, those attained in the past, but with fewer bureaucratic building materials.

A third trend, which is much more tentative, is the phenomenon of governments trying to pursue by stealth objectives that are formally proscribed, for instance by democratic agreements or international arrangements such as the European Common Market. When this happens, the 'obvious' or straightforward tools for realising 'unmentionable' aims, such as import restrictions or pay controls, have to be left aside. Instead governments delve into their tool-boxes for instruments to use out of context in pursuit of what may be an unacknowledgeable purpose.

I will come back to this 'rummage-bag' phenomenon later in the book. Governments have always used such tactics, of course, but the need at least to pay lip-service to growing 'internationalisation' and 'participative democracy' may well herald an increasing tendency to act in this way. Thus it is all the more important to be equipped to look closely at the instruments that governments are actually using rather that what they say they believe in.

These are just some of the reasons why it is worth looking into government's tool-kit, and all of them will be pursued later in the book. I am not, of course, suggesting that other possible ways of looking at 'what government does' do not have pay-offs, too. But they do not have *these pay-offs.*

The focus and limits of the book

To focus on government's tool-kit, we need lenses which necessarily distort other aspects of government. This is unavoidable in any kind of inquiry; and it is important to be clear about it in order to prevent confusion or false expectations. Three points especially need to be stressed.

Focusing on the government–society interface

First, the book explores the tools used by government *only* at the interface between government and society, as was shown in Figure 1.1. That is the point at which 'they' (governments) meet 'us' (citizens or subjects). The book says nothing about the tools used *within* government to control and co-ordinate its own far-flung activities and agencies.

Exactly where the government–society interface is, of course, depends on how you choose to define the boundaries of government, and here that is deliberately left somewhat imprecise. In reality, of course, that interface is often extremely fuzzy. There are learned and sophisticated discussions in many countries about the extent to which government is 'colonised' by the non-government sector and vice versa, so that the boundaries are very blurred. This can happen at a much more down-to-earth administrative level, too. Again, there are well known puzzles as to whether one locates organisations such as defence-contracting firms or 'parastatal' bodies as part of 'government' or not.

Such disputes are far from trivial, but they belong to a different kind of discussion. For the purpose of exploring government's tool-kit, it does not matter much what the answers to these questions are, because where exactly you decide to draw the boundary between government and the world outside affects only the overall proportions in which government tools are used, not the basic elements themselves. For us, it is sufficient to adopt the naive perspective of the man in the street who believes that there is a clear distinction between governments and the rest of humanity, and that government is what 'they' do to 'us'.

Treating government as a totality

Second, the book looks at government in general and as a totality. This too is a simplification of something that is very complicated in reality. The approach is general in the sense that it does not necessarily refer to any particular government or level of government. The tools that are discussed are generic to government. They are used in every country; most of them are common not only in the present day, but go back far into the past.

Moreover, Government is treated here – to begin with, at least – as a totality. Everyone knows that 'in reality' government consists of a host of different 'cells' or agencies, often squabbling and at cross purposes with one another. But once again it is sufficient for us to adopt as a starting point the perspective of the man in the street who does not divide government into its many component parts or agencies, but rather sees 'officialdom' as a whole – a monolith. I shall come to 'disaggregation' later on.

'Unlearning' conventional descriptions of government activity

Thinking of government as a totality and ignoring all the 'office politics' and other processes which go on inside it may well involve some degree of mental re-adjustment or 'unlearning' of what we already know. A third kind of 'unlearning' that is required – difficult, but equally necessary if we are to concentrate on government's tool-kit – is to forget everything we know about how government *itself* describes its activities.

The reason for this is that governments tend to describe their activities officially in terms of purposes or fields of concern, not instruments, and it is very important not to confuse the two. When governments draw up budgets, the headings tend to be descriptions of purposes (especially in 'modern' budgeting systems). When they divide their tasks into agencies, the boundaries tend – at least at the topmost level – to reflect the purposes being pursued. It is for this reason that we can easily come to think of purposes or fields of activity (defence, health, education, etc.) as the 'natural' way of describing what government does.

But if we want to think in terms of tools or instruments, we must deviate from the conventional way of thinking both negatively and positively. First, negatively, we must unlearn preconceived categories based on the purposes of government. Identifying a set of tools is quite different from listing government's interests or purposes – our second possible way of answering the 'plain man's question'. A tool can often be used for many different purposes or applications. Think of the axe in the hands of the fireman, the forester, the executioner; or the mallet in the hands of the Boy Scout, the shoemaker, the judge. Indeed, it has already been pointed out that a tool can often be taken right out of context and used for some purpose quite other than that for which it is ostensibly designed: that is something that happens quite often in government.

Second, positively, if there is no satisfactory, ready-made official language for describing government's tool-kit, we must invent our own. It goes without saying that most government officials going about their daily tasks no more 'see' those tasks in terms of detectors and effectors or of the components of the 'NATO' scheme than Molière's M. Vautrin conceived of himself as speaking prose. And when the eight kinds of basic government tool that have already been outlined are further subdivided later in the book, other terms will have to be contrived to denote the devices involved. Some of these names may seem infelicitous, but they are only labels: the reader is quite welcome to substitute his or her own terms. What *does* need to be stressed is that the labels that are used to describe government's tools do not spring from a mere love of neologism, but from the absence of any existing coherent official usage which would serve the purpose. Since government's tools do not come with labels on them, we must work out our own language.

Finally, this book says nothing about whether government's tools *ought* to be used extensively or modestly – whether government ought to be 'interventionist' or *laissez-faire*. An agnostic stance is deliberately taken on such matters. The book is addressed to readers of both persuasions.

Where do we go from here?

So much for the whys and wherefores. You now need a quick sketch of the course that the book takes from here. The book has three parts, each of which is introduced by a few paragraphs describing the themes or ideas to be discussed.

Parts I and II attempt to lay out the tool-kit, building on the basic components that have already been described and summarised in Figures 1.1 and 1.2. Part I outlines and discusses government's effecting tools, and Part II, somewhat more briefly, does the same for detectors.

Part III looks at the tool-box as a whole, and in a more analytic way. It picks up markers that are laid down in Parts I and II. It shows how a comparatively simple conception of government's tools can be used as an analytic device, as a means for reducing the apparent complexity of government operations to a comprehensible level. Government's tools or instruments – in one sense extremely diverse and 'all around us' – can be made comparatively simple by 'reading' them as permutations, refinements and variations on a listed number of basic types.

One can look at it the other way round, too. Chapter 7 shows how, if we take even a very limited number of basic instruments and then start to think of combining them into mixes, the combinations can start to run away with us, creating staggering variety (in the sense of number of possible states). That chapter also takes up the discussion of how we can use a 'tool-kit' conception of government to think in terms of alternatives, to make comparisons and to monitor changes over time.

Government's tools are, of course, potentially dangerous. Like most tools, they are benign or malign according to the purpose of the user. Many tools can be used as weapons. All of government's tools, even the most innocent-seeming of them, can be used as instruments of repression. Their application therefore raises hot moral issues as well as what at first sight may seem to be more neutral questions of economy and effectiveness. Chapter 8 looks at this theme, considering some of the ways in which we might judge government's choice and application of its tools. The chapter demonstrates the practical impossibility of applying any mechanistic form of rationality to the choice of 'mixes' of government tools, and shows some of the complexities which in reality attend even so apparently unexceptionable an idea as 'using bureaucracy sparingly'.

Finally, Chapter 9 considers the way in which governments may change their mix of tools over time. How does the mix change when circumstances change? Has there been a shift from the 'regulatory state' to the 'manipulative state'? Is there any evidence to suggest that, in countries like the United Kingdom and the USA, there has been a shift from direct government operations to money-moving operations, or 'government by cheque-book'? In what ways can government's tools be misapplied or overloaded?

First, then, let us take a look at government's effecting tools – the means by which it tries to influence the world outside.

[illegible]

[illegible] BROWNE [illegible]

[illegible] and Everything [illegible]

[illegible]

[illegible]

[illegible]

here is 'particular' only in the fairly weak sense that each customer selects items from the store in accordance with his or her particular requirements – rather like those 'pick your own' stores or market gardens which invite us to select and collect the individual items that we want to buy instead of having them ready packaged.

A somewhat more 'particular' form of the 'prompted query response' is individual counselling and advice. Government counselling for farmers is one of the best known and longest established applications, and the same principle is now widely used in relation to business firms. Other applications include individualised advice to consumers on their legal rights, rehabilitation advice to ex-convicts who wish to 'go straight', advice on contraception or marital conflict, and 'dial-a-counsellor' services.

Government's 'nodality' may equip it well for giving out information in this way, on the basis of the many different cases which it sees. It may thus be able to act as a broker in information even if it has no ideas of its own at all. Moreover, such brokerage may offer a convenient way of interspersing technical information, for which there is a real demand – to the extent that outsiders are prepared to come to government for counselling – with persuasion of a rather less neutral type.

Direct notification

The two kinds of 'bespoke message' that have been discussed so far are both *responses*. The information-dispenser has to be 'triggered' from outside, by the informee. The other way to convey such a message is for government to make the approach itself, not even pretending to 'wait to be asked'. This device can be called *direct notification*. When government uses direct notification, its subjects do not need to seek for information or to maintain a look out.

Applications of direct notification range from relatively mundane messages to more fundamental ones. An example of the first is the reminder sent to us by the government to inform us that our vehicle licence, dog licence, or whatever is about to expire. Examples of the second are the letter or telegram sent by government to inform the next of kin of a soldier's death, or the direct visit by government officials, as when police knock on individual house doors to warn of a gas leak or a dangerous animal on the loose.

The advantage of direct notification is obvious. It is the most certain way for government to get a message across to the very individuals it wishes to reach. Government has little alternative but to use this device when it is trying to communicate with people who are illiterate, apathetic, generally incompetent, socially isolated or who do not speak the language of the country. The disadvantage is equally obvious: the device can take a heavy toll of government's resources if large numbers of people have to be approached separately with a message tailor-made for each individual case. Indeed, if all government messages had to be delivered in this way, instead of the very exceptional ones, informing the public at large would become an extremely expensive and laborious process.

Group-targeted messages

The opposite of a bespoke message, of course, is a standard message which is beamed at the world at large, and this type is considered in the next section. But there is also an important in-between type: that is, the message which government directs to a particular group rather than to somebody or to anybody. This can be termed the *group-targeted message*.

Like bespoke messages, 'group-targeted' messages can come in several forms. Sometimes, government may use a 'reply' as the outlet for its information, like the bespoke 'query responses' discussed earlier. An example might be a government-stated press conference, when a specified group – perhaps a group that has been 'vetted' – is invited to seek enlightenment (if that is what it is) from government.

Sometimes, on the other hand, government may direct its message at groups on the 'direct notification' principle. For example, most governments send official publicity material which depicts their regime in a favourable light, publicises goods available from the country or investment opportunities for foreign firms, to selected individuals and organisations who are supposedly influential in other countries. Government frequently uses similar techniques on its home ground, when it seeks to harness 'opinion leaders' as part of an information campaign.

These examples are cases of groups being used as intermediaries for the wider transmission of a government message. But on occasions the group itself may be the final target. For example, in Britain the Department of Health and Social Security approaches its aim of reducing the overall cost of drugs supplied through the government health service by sending information packs to doctors involved in the service. The information is not 'personalised' to each doctor, as it would be if government were using 'direct notification': it is directed to doctors as a group. The idea is that the information packs will enable doctors to identify less expensive alternatives to the brands of medicine that are most heavily advertised by commercial drug manufacturers and wholesalers, and are thus most likely to come to a doctor's notice. Since government pays the bulk of the cost of the drugs that are prescribed by doctors, it has a clear interest in laying such information before them.

Targeting information to, and through, groups is a basic stand-by for any publicist, not only for government. Using groups for diffusing a message has the advantage of relative economy; it is perhaps the social equivalent of the spreading of plant seeds through the medium of birds, by the production of attractive, edible berries. The device is widespread in modern government, given the importance of news media and of powerful pressure groups seeking to act as 'opinion leaders'.

'Broadcast' messages

The opposite of a 'bespoke message' to an individual is a general message to the world at large or to whomever it may concern. The latter can be termed *broadcast messages*, but broadcasting must here be understood in a wide sense, with no necessary reference to radio or television transmission.

Three main types of 'broadcast messages' can be distinguished. The first is here termed, for want of a better word, the *privished message*. 'Privishing' is a word sometimes used in publishing, meaning to publish something in such a way that it remains relatively 'private', i.e. confined to a small circle. The term is used here to denote the kind of message which government gives to the world at large in such a way that anyone who takes the trouble or knows the code may gain access to the information. But the message is propagated in such a way that it requires some degree of effort on the part of the informee to 'tune in': it needs active decoding or is transmitted in a form that is not designed to reach the uninformed or uninitiated.

There are a number of ways that a message can be 'privished' while ostensibly being made freely available. For example, a publication can be put on general sale, but at such a high price that very few people will buy it. An obscure medium may be used, such as a small ad in a specialist journal or official gazette rather than an attention-grabbing advertisement on television at peak viewing time or a full-page spread in a popular daily newspaper. Or the message may be made so cryptic that even when transmitted through a general information medium, only a few people will know the code necessary to read it – as happens with those St Valentine's Day messages published in the small ad columns of the newspapers.

Many of government's messages are 'privished', for good or bad reasons. One example is government's sea-marks and lighthouses, which send out messages to whomever it may concern. To actually read the message, however, requires some degree of training and application on the part of the informee. A similar example is government weather reports for seamen: in the United Kingdom, such reports are transmitted through a general-purpose radio station, but to understand them you need to know where the government's weather stations are and what the numbers being reported refer to. Government's 'published' details of patent applications – compressed technical jargon in an official gazette – are a further example. Where there is a clearly defined specialist audience, 'privishing' may be quite sufficient to reach government's intended informees. It all depends, of course, on the degree of attentiveness of the audience.

Packaged self-serve messages

Somewhat less 'exclusive' than the 'privished message' is what we can call the *packaged self-serve message*. As the name implies, government is here using the methods of the self-service store or restaurant to convey a package of information to whomever it may concern. In contrast to the 'privished message', much less is required of the informee, but this mode still requires outsiders to take some initiative to obtain the proffered package. It is the approach of the dating agency which invites you to pick your mate from 5,000 photographs rather than the one which offers candidates suitable to you personally after a screening process (which is a 'bespoke message'). The information is not personalised in any way. It is standard, packaged, pre-selected and available to anyone who chooses to take the trouble to pick it up.

Government, like every large organisation, goes to great lengths to pre-package standard information, the availability of which may well be heavily advertised in order to attract customers. The 'package' can take many forms, for example leaflets, exhibitions, brochures, tapes, recorded telephone messages. The advantage of this approach is that it may reduce the need for bespoke messages, which typically require considerable effort and expense to convey. But, like privished messages, self-serve information will only be effective if the prospective informees are sufficiently interested to want to help themselves to the packages on offer.

Propaganda

Much, if not all, of government's information output can be seen as 'propaganda' in the sense that it is designed to persuade or to structure the informee's perception rather than to convey purely neutral or technical information. Propaganda in *that* sense has a very long history, going back at least as far as Pope Gregory XV's *Congregatio de Propaganda Fidei* of 1622 (Zijderveld, 1979, p. 68). But the term *propaganda* is used here more narrowly, to denote the kind of general information for which government does not wait to be asked, but rather seeks to press upon the world at large. When it uses propaganda, government speaks to its subjects in such a way that the large-print, voluble message is forced down the public's throat willy-nilly. The message is standard and aimed at a mass audience. No investment of effort or knowledge is required before the message can be read or obtained, in contrast to privished or self-serve messages.

Government propaganda in this sense is common enough. Even under relatively liberal regimes, the public at large may be bombarded with general government exhortations and warnings – to save petrol or electricity, join the army, beware of the ill-effects of tobacco, avoid dropping litter, give blood, drive safely, lock up valuables, avoid using electric lawnmowers when the grass is wet, etc. We, the public, do not seek this kind of government information deliberately. It seeks us.

Governments have always used propaganda, although modern media have changed its style. Perhaps the first mass propaganda campaign in the modern style by the British government came in the 1870s, when handbills addressed to the public at large (advertising the Savings Bank) were dropped through every letter-box in the country (Clark, 1971, p. 23). Since then, of course, mass-propaganda techniques have changed enormously, especially with the development of psychological warfare (Brown, 1963, p. 87).

Government propaganda can vary widely in the directness of the message being conveyed. Sometimes that message is immediately recognisable and self-consciously conveyed through a conventional communications medium in the traditional 'agitprop' style. The set-piece government broadcast, the poster or leaflet campaign, the large-scale newspaper advertisement are all *cliché* propaganda weapons, employed by every government from time to time.

On the other hand, there are also less straightforward, more subtle ways for government to press a message on the public at large. It may intersperse persuasion with an ostensibly neutral or technical message, as anyone can discover by listening to and comparing the news broadcasts that are put out by the radio stations of the competing world powers. It may sugar the pill by slipping its message into an apparently quite untainted source. This is the reason why Lenin believed cinema films to be the ideal vehicle for political persuasion (Jarvie, 1970, p. 57). Even in Britain, the long-running BBC radio soap opera *The Archers* was at one time used as a vehicle for government persuasion, particularly for the farming community (Ogilvy-Webb, 1965, p. 113). Indeed, there is perhaps a tendency in Western countries for government to move away from the old-fashioned mass-propaganda techniques of a more palpable kind and to move instead in this kind of direction.

The tool-set in context

Having picked out a handful of ways in which government can use information as an 'effecting' tool, the second part of this chapter considers how the overall mix of these information-dispensers may vary from one case to another and what circumstances are likely to affect the mix. The discussion begins with comparisons, combinations and substitutions, and concludes by looking at the circumstances that are likely to govern the use of the different kinds of messages considered here.

Comparisons

Our seven sub-types of information-dispensing tools are all in common use by government, though not necessarily by every government agency. Indeed, the production of propaganda tends to be concentrated in specialised agencies, such as the International Communications Agency – the somewhat uncommunicative name of the US government's overseas propaganda office. Moreover, the job of dispensing information to the outside world is often concentrated in specialised units *within* a government agency; not every official uses these tools (Fagen, 1966, pp. 131–2, n. 5). As was mentioned earlier, every large organisation has its all-purpose inquiry office to field or to ward off unexpected inquiries, its press office to 'manage' the news media, its batteries of PR men, image-makers and flak-catchers.

Each government agency tends to have its characteristic 'profile', in terms of the types of information-dispenser that it uses. Government agricultural agencies, as we have seen, often emphasise prompted query responses as their leading information tool, through advice and counselling services offered to individual farmers. Propaganda to the public at large is usually more peripheral to their activities, but will certainly be used on occasion, for example in campaigns to prevent the spread of animal diseases such as rabies. By contrast, an energy-conservation agency may very well put a heavy weight on propaganda, exhorting the public at large to save fuel in a variety of ways. A central bank might lean more in the direction of privishing or of group-targeted messages; a job placement agency might rely on prompted query responses or packaged self-serve messages. It is rare to find two agencies employing an identical mix.

Combinations and permutations

It would, of course, be easy to expand the number of sub-types of information-disseminating tools well beyond the seven that have been considered here. For the sake of simplicity, that will not be done here. But even a relatively small number of basic elements, if they are free to combine, can produce a wealth of 'hybrids'. There are in fact about 5,000 logically possible combinations of the seven kinds of message discussed here. Government can combine these instruments in several ways.

First, it can combine several types of information-dispenser *simultaneously*, so that they reinforce one another. For example, when there is an outbreak of cattle plague or an epidemic, or if a major change in social behaviour is required (such as a switch from driving on the left to driving on the right or the introduction of a new currency system), government may want to pull out all the stops, and is likely to employ every means available to put its message across. It may track down particular individuals who have been exposed to infection in order to warn them of their danger, mount special approaches to inform members of relevant groups, and at the same time launch a propaganda campaign in the hope of alerting the general public. Even in less extreme cases – for example when government interests itself in 'protecting the consumer' – a variety of information-dispensers are commonly linked together.

Second, government can combine its information-dispensers in time, by using them *in sequence*. Once the public's attention has been caught by propaganda, it may be possible to offer further information by different means. For example, if government wants to set up a lottery, it may seek to attract customers by propaganda in the form of widespread popular advertising, stressing the large prizes to be won. Those who are 'hooked' by such a message may then be informed further by the self-serve method, inviting them to pick up the leaflet which describes the scheme in more detail. For those who are lucky enough to win a prize, the mode may then switch to privished messages or to direct notification, depending on how the winners are to learn of their success. Even then, government may well need at least one further information-dispenser to handle unclaimed prizes or untraceable winners.

Two other types of combination are possible. One is a combination in both space *and* time, involving a larger number of possible arrays. The other is a combination of the various kinds of information-dispenser with the other classes of government's 'effecting' and 'detecting' tools, which were introduced in Chapter 1.

Tools for propagating information, for example, are commonly linked to tools for obtaining it, i.e. government detectors. When government requests or demands information from its subjects there is often an accompanying propaganda campaign explaining why the information is needed. Failure to send in a compulsory return may trigger a reminder from government, directly notifying the individual offender; or those who have difficulty in completing the returns may be referred to such-and-such an explanatory leaflet, on the self-serve principle. The inquiry office producing prompted or unprompted query responses is invariably a two-way street in information traffic. When we start to think of coupling information-dispensers with government's other classes of tools, the number of possible combinations takes a quantum jump, from thousands to billions.

Information-dispensers as substitutes for other government tools

Not only can government's tools be combined with one another; sometimes they can be substituted for one another, too. Governments often change from one instrument to another as they try to perform a certain task. As with combinations of instruments, government can substitute one type of information outlet for another, or substitute between information output in general and its other main types of 'effecting' tools.

As an example of the first type of substitution it was suggested earlier that government attempts to influence the population at large in many countries have shifted to some extent from the general propaganda mode, so popular in the 1940s, to the use of a more selective, group-targeted approach: manipulating the news media and treating them as a theatre in which government seeks to appear in a dominant and favourable role (Clark, 1971). This kind of 'theatrocracy' (Lyman and Scott, 1975, quoted in Sennett, 1977) requires government continually to stage-manage spectaculars and pseudo-events that will eat up media time and attention.

Another case of a shift from one kind of information outlet to another can be taken from the British government's job placement service. Until comparatively recently, government offered information to job-seekers in its employment exchanges by means of a personal interview, in which an official suggested those job vacancies that might be suitable to each interviewee, depending on the particular circumstances of each case. This bespoke, 'prompted query response' approach is now supplemented by a 'packaged self-serve' approach, in which lists of job vacancies are displayed in government offices for any job-seeker to scrutinise.

Not only may one type of information outlet sometimes be substitutable for another, but information dissemination in general may also sometimes turn out to be substitutable for other classes of government 'effector'. For instance, it is often cheaper for government to inform than to order, forbid, bribe or coerce. Standard examples are road safety and anti-smoking propaganda and other types of information which government aims at the public at large to encourage 'healthy living' – propaganda which, if successful, may lessen the load on other types of government instruments, such as payment for the medical treatment of victims of preventable diseases or accidents.

Sometimes government may substitute information for other kinds of 'effecting' tools in less familiar contexts. In Britain, government added propaganda to its armoury of weapons for dealing with strikes for the first time in 1919, when it responded to a railway strike with a massive propaganda campaign directed at the public at large (Martin, 1980). Another case arose after an increased and much-publicised degree of refusal among the populace to co-operate with the 1971 census (*Security of the Census of Population*, 1973, p. 15). The government then mounted a much bigger propaganda campaign about the alleged social benefits to be gained from government census-taking in time for the subsequent census in 1981 – a campaign that was intended to lessen the degree to which government would have to use coercive instruments against individuals who refused to answer its census questions. Similarly, the British government turned increasingly to the financing of consumer advice centres in the 1970s, because telling consumers about their legal rights and advising them on individual cases began to be seen as a more effective way of seeing that laws on trading standards were carried out than the more traditional government detection method of concentrating on periodic rota inspections of retail stores by government officials (Cranston, 1979).

Even further removed from the standard example of health and safety propaganda is the case of public order policing. Modern police forces in large cities have powerful tools available to them for exercising authority over turbulent crowds and rioters. These tools are applications of 'organisation', which will be discussed in Chapter 5. But the police may well prefer on occasion to lay these tools aside in order to appear to be struggling against heavy odds in the eyes of the general public. By doing this, insurgents rather than the police may be portrayed as the bully-boys and the police can gain the public relations advantage with the general public who are watching the event on their television screens. (As Rollo, 1980 has pointed out, a further tactic is to add plain-clothes police *agents provocateurs*, to ensure that the crowd's behaviour does in fact reach unpopular excesses.)

A well known British case in which the manipulation of information was to some extent substituted for more direct action was the Grunwick affair of 1976–8 (Rogaly, 1977). This was a labour dispute which developed into a spectacular mass picket by trade-union sympathisers outside the gates of the Grunwick film-processing factory in North London. The conflict reached its peak in the summer of 1977, during which time the number of pickets attending approached 20,000 on some days.

This number presented no real challenge to a police force equipped with modern anti-riot equipment such as water cannon and tear gas. But rather than use hardware of this kind – which would inevitably have cast the pickets in the role of underdogs in the eyes of the television-watching public – the police chose to fight the Grunwick pickets in front of the television cameras on terms which made the forces of authority appear to be in constant danger of defeat at the hands of a threatening army of insurgents, and attracted sympathetic publicity to the injuries of policemen and police horses. Indeed, the former Commissioner of Metropolitan Police, Sir Robert Mark, remarked of the Grunwick affair that: 'The real art of policing a modern mass democracy is to win by appearing to lose' (quoted in Dromey and Taylor, 1978, p. 136) – in other words, to treat policing as an exercise in manipulating the mass media.

Substitution of one class of government tools for another is something that we will come across again in later chapters. Indeed, as was mentioned in the last chapter, one of the advantages of looking at government in a 'tool-kit' perspective is precisely that it sensitises us to look for possibilities for substitution. Often there are more alternatives open to government than might at first sight appear.

Types of information-dispenser: 'protases' or 'precipitating conditions'

Finally, what circumstances might affect the type of information outlet – or mix of outlets – that government uses? When would we expect each tool to be used? Many things might affect this, but here only four main elements will be discussed. They are the size of population, the degree of attention, the technical/persuasive mix of information content, and the extent to which government rules with the broad consensus of its subjects.

(1) *Size of population.* The relative cost to government of particular as against general messages is likely to depend on the size of the informee population. When that population is very small, it may be no more costly to use particular messages than to use general ones, and indeed the latter might well tax government's bureaucratic resources more heavily than the former. But there is a cross-over point, and particular messages are likely to become much more expensive to government when the informee population becomes large.

This tells us something about the limitations of the particular message.

Examples were given earlier to show that 'bespoke' messages are used quite commonly by government. Government could scarcely do without them. But nor could government rely on this type of message for *all* its information dissemination. The disadvantages of doing so are obvious enough. For example, giving out *all* of government's information by waiting for unpredictable and heterogeneous inquiries and then delivering tailor-made responses according to the circumstances of each particular case, would be enormously expensive. It would require armies of high-grade officials capable of fielding – or skilfully blocking – an enormous range of possible inquiries. It would be like a railway which declined to publish or display any timetables, so that each single prospective traveller had to be told personally about trains and times for his or her particular trip. 'Direct notification', where government actually tracks down each informee, may also take a heavy toll of government's bureaucratic resources when the population to be informed is large.

By and large, then, government is likely to try to confine bespoke messages to relatively small informee populations, extreme situations, or to a back-up or long-stop role – just as a real railway will usually maintain some kind of bespoke inquiry facility to back up its general messages. When the informee population is large, government is likely to look to 'broadcast' or 'group-targeted' messages. It will try to prepackage information in some way, before a mass of inquirers actually turns up on its doorstep.

(2) *Degree of attention.* A second element that is likely to affect the mixture of information-propagating tools is the degree of *attention* that is manifested by the informee population. Where attention is high, government need not employ tools such as direct notification and propaganda, any more than a business firm with eager customers need resort to heavy advertising of its products. Its subjects will look for information, triggering unprompted query responses and being alert for privished messages. Little 'spoon-feeding' of information will be necessary.

Attention is, of course, a function of interest and specialism. When our interest is focused on a certain topic, for example our occupational specialism, scarce goods or services that we wish to obtain, prizes that we hope to win, our other interests and hobbies, then we will be highly receptive to messages within that field. We may well be on a 'rumour circuit' which informs us of approaching events long before any formal announcement is made. When the relevant group or individual is hanging on government's every word, it is a waste of effort for government to 'shout' or to buttonhole its listener. It need only whisper or let slip the most cryptic hint into the information network for the message to gain immediate currency. But government will find that it needs to move more in the direction of direct notification and propaganda when it is operating outside or cutting across established information networks, or when it is trying to reach individuals who are not consciously involved in the matter in question. The whispering gallery effect ceases to operate.

For example, there was no need for the British government to go to great lengths to announce Queen Victoria's death in 1901 to the citizens of London, who were mostly 'tuned in' to the royal happenings through direct observation, rumour and newspapers. But the government had to send a special gunboat to proclaim the Queen's death to the remote Scottish island of St Kilda (the inhabitants of which had been unaware of Queen Victoria's accession for a year after she came to the throne in 1837 (Steel, 1975, pp. 33–4)). And degree of attention is not, of course, only or necessarily related to geographical remoteness.

(3) *Technical/persuasive mix*. An element that is likely to be closely related to the degree of attention is the mix of technical as against persuasive content in government's messages. In general, the higher the technical element and the lower the 'selling' element in the message, the more likely it is that government's subjects will seek out the information in the 'privished', 'self-serve' or 'prompted query response' mode – perhaps to the extent even of paying for the message, as in the case of government maps or other documents sold in government bookshops, or even government counselling services on some matters.

There is usually a mix because in many cases government information is not neatly divisible into 'technical' and 'persuasive'. Often a fine balance has to be obtained, interspersing persuasion with technicalities in such a way that the message still attracts demand and thus does not oblige government to use propaganda or direct notification methods. Government advisory services operating on the prompted query response principle, for example, typically combine proselytising with more neutral information.

Of course, what is 'technical' and what is 'persuasive' is not entirely an objective matter. To a considerable extent it lies in the eye of the beholder. Where one observer sees a factual piece of information, another will perceive hidden messages, unspoken assumptions, significant exclusions. For example, if government seeks to inform teenagers about the use of contraceptives – as did the British government in 1981 – this may seem to some as no more than 'technical' information, but others will see it as an official encouragement to promiscuity ('MINISTRIES ENCOURAGE YOUNG SEX', blared *The Daily Telegraph* of 14 October 1981). Nor is this just a question of difference between one individual and another. It may be related to the final element to be discussed here, i.e. the general social climate within which government operates.

(4) *The wider social context.* What is likely to be the effect of the general social context within which government operates on the type of information outlets that it uses? 'Wider social context' is used here to mean the extent to which government operates in a context of consensus or of general acceptance on the part of its subjects or citizens. In general it may be supposed that, as the degree of that consensus or general acceptance declines, the emphasis will shift in the direction of propaganda and unprompted query responses – and possibly of direct notification, too.

This is because government's subjects may be expected to be less inclined to take up 'advertised' information from the authorities when their loyalty and trust in government declines. But at the same time they may be more inclined to find out government's secrets and to press it for information which it is not eager to give out in a pre-packaged form, or indeed in any form. To the extent that the public at large displays increasing attention and interest in information which government is trying to hide, more load may be thrown on the unprompted query response form of information outlet – a device which, as was noted before, is expensive for government to use in large quantities.

Just as a social context of 'low consensus' will cause attention on the part of the public to increase in relation to some kinds of information – the kind government wants to hide – that attention will *decrease* in relation to the messages that government actually wants to put across. Those information outlets that rely on 'take up' by the public, such as self-serve or prompted-query methods, will prove less effective. Even groups such as the news media or pressure groups may become less reliable and amenable as information conduits. Government may therefore find increasing pressure to use the propaganda instrument in an attempt to put its message across in a general way. Of course, in a context of declining consensus or acceptability, even this instrument may come to have diminishing or negative returns. Credibility sinks to the point where anything that government chooses to say to the public at large is ignored or automatically dismissed as lies. If government really wants to get a message across, it may have to inform each person individually, using direct notification – another very expensive way for government to dispense information in large quantities, as we have already noted.

Hence, at the very point where it might be most important for government to communicate effectively with its subjects, it is likely to be both over-informing and under-informing them, snowing them under with propaganda while at the same time blocking their demands to know its secrets through unprompted queries. It is likely to be increasingly thrown back on its most 'expensive' information outlets. Indeed, there is a point of social pressure at which government is likely to switch the emphasis away from information and to lay more emphasis on its other main effecting tools.

Conclusion

This chapter began by trying to convey some idea of the staggering variety of information that modern government purveys to its subjects – from the ponderous to the trivial, from the abstruse to the direct. It only takes a casual look round a government bookshop to underline the point. Information from government is not only a form of 'effecting' tool that we find in use all around us; it often comes early in the sequence of government's responses to a problem. For instance, one of the British government's first moves on the outbreak of war in 1914 was to appoint a Director of Propaganda (Clark, 1971, p. 24), one of the US government's first responses to the suppression of trade unions in Poland in 1981 was to stage a one-hour television spectacular entitled 'Let Poland be Poland'.

Using information as an effector has the advantage of not necessarily laying government's authority on the line. 'When arguments are used, authority is left in abeyance' (Arendt, quoted in Wrong, 1979, p. 32) and the same might be said of information dispensation in a broader sense. But in many situations, of course, there comes a point at which other instruments must be used – orders, threats, bribes, physical coercion. Mere communications – words – are not enough. We now need to explore other kinds of effecting tools.

3 'Treasure' and Cheque-Book Government

Thus much of this will make black white, foul fair,
Wrong right, base noble, old young, coward valiant.
. . .Why, this
Will lug your priests and servants from your sides,
Pluck stout men's pillows from below their heads:
This yellow slave
Will knit and break religions, bless the accursed,
Make the hoar leprosy adored, place thieves
And give them title, knee and approbation.

(Shakespeare, *Timon of Athens*, Act III, Scene III; substantially the same passage is quoted by Marx and Engels, 1968, pp. 262–3)

After 'nodality', government's second basic resource is 'treasure'. As was explained in Chapter 1, this denotes government's stock of 'fungible chattels', in the sense of anything that can be freely exchanged.

Of course, almost anything can be exchanged in some circumstances, and thus 'treasure' certainly overlaps at the margin with other resources of government that can be used for trade or exchange – such as official licences or certificates, pieces of information, or anything else in the gift of government that is 'as good as money in the bank' to someone. But the discussion in this chapter is limited to what is *freely* exchangeable – moneys or money-like substances.

The reader needs no lengthy demonstration of the power of 'treasure' in the hand of government, and so this chapter will be very short. The official pen can sometimes be as mighty as the sword, especially when it is signing cheques. Treasure is what enables government to exchange, to buy favours, to court popularity, to hire mercenaries (see Lasswell and Kaplan, 1950, pp. 90–1). The power of treasure, dramatised in the epigraph to this chapter, is a subject of endless fascination. As F. P.

Dunne's Mr. Dooley observed, 'The American nation is a fine people . . . They love th' eagle . . . on the back iv a dollar' (Dunne, 1899, p. 222).

Governments have found it worthwhile to amass treasure since early times, and using treasure is an everyday feature of modern government. Government's guineas find their way into almost every domain of our lives, and in many countries literally from the cradle to the grave: from the maternity benefits that accompany our birth to the death benefits that follow our death. Rose and Peters (1978, ch. 3, pp. 65–85) have shown that in Western countries almost everyone gets his or her spoon into government's financial gravy at some point in their lives.

This is not just a matter of welfare payments. Government is the biggest single purchaser in many countries, buying everything from boots and shoes to currencies. Weidenbaum (1969, pp. 11, 35) points out that purchases of goods and services from the private sector overtook wage payments to its own employees as the largest single category in the US federal government's budget after the Second World War, and that in the 1960s the federal government was buying over three and a half million separate items.

There are many other ways in which government can put its money to work. It may offer grants or concessionary rate loans for a wide variety of purposes: for example, for moving a business to a certain favoured area, for building and equipping factories, for converting from oil-fired boilers to coal. It may offer subsidies: for example, on exports, on agricultural produce, on fuel for favoured users such as farmers or fishermen. It may offer payments of a venal or less mentionable kind: for example, Stockwell (1978, p. 246) observes that 'The US government, through the CIA, disburses tens of millions of dollars each year in cash bribes.' This is, in short, an age of cheque-book government.

This chapter will briefly review some of the ways in which government can use its treasure as an instrument to try to influence the world outside, and then set 'money-moving' in a wider context. Once again, we can look at 'particular' and 'general' applications of treasure, beginning with the particular.

Customised payments

Government can use its treasure in two main ways. It can exchange it for some good or service. Or it can 'give it away', without requiring any further *quid pro quo* (or promise of such), to those whom it considers deserving, whose favours it wishes to buy, or who meet stipulated eligibility criteria. These uses can be hard to separate at the margin, and some specific methods foı conveying treasure – grants and loans, for example – can be used in either way.

Similarly, government can give away its treasure in a highly particularised way – where the identity of the specific payee is crucial – or in a general way, where payment is made to those whom it may concern, with identity not of the essence. 'Particularising' can also relate in some cases to the degree to which the manner of payment is one-off or specially contrived, even where the identity of the payee is not actually known – as in the extreme case where an (anonymous) blackmailer requires us to leave the money he demands in the form of used banknotes of stipulated denominations in a certain telephone box or hollow tree.

'Particular' forms of conveying treasure can be termed *customised payments*, and some such payments are indeed not far from the blackmailer example, in that they have to be elaborately tailored to the circumstances of a particular individual. Government may need to use such methods for handing over money demanded by a hi-jacker or terrorist in return for the release of hostages. It occasionally chooses to disburse treasure by elaborate ceremonies, by which payment is made in a special and formalised manner. For example, in 1981 US President Reagan personally presented a specially made outsize federal government cheque for $85 million to Mayor Koch of New York City. And there are less dramatic circumstances in which government payments may have to be highly 'particularised': for example, if police give 'first aid' money to cover the immediate needs of a person who has been robbed in the middle of the night.

Contracts

The term *contracts* can serve to denote payments that are 'customised or particular in the sense that they are paid to some specific individual or organisation, and at the same time conditional in that they are made in exchange for some direct *quid pro quo*, the recipient being required to supply, produce or promise something. Sometimes the *quid pro quo* required may be a promise *not* to produce – a device satirised by Heller in *Catch-22*:

> The government paid him well for every bushel of alfalfa he did not

grow. The more alfalfa he did not grow, the more money the government gave him, and he spent every penny he didn't earn on new land to increase the amount of alfalfa he did not produce. (Heller, 1969, p. 94)

Government constantly uses contracts for purposes both trivial and grave. As has already been mentioned, it is a buyer, lender and granter on a huge scale. It uses contracts both to encourage its subjects to do things that they may already be predisposed to do (such as improving their houses) and to do things that they would not otherwise dream of doing in the absence of government offers of payment (such as processing nuclear waste). It may use contracts to 'distance' itself from operations in which it does not wish to appear too closely involved. For example, Stockwell (1978, p. 56) describes how private charter firms may be used to transport stocks of foreign weapons to groups overseas in cases where the US government wishes to mask its presence, and comments, 'even tighter security can be obtained by contracting with international dealers who will purchase arms in Europe and subcontract independently to have them flown into the target area'.

The term 'contracts' is used here as a generic word to cover all payments made to a specific payee and with strings attached. Payments that are termed 'grants' or 'loans' would be included to the extent that government, in making such payments, requires conditions to be met, rather than offering a free gift or a no-strings loan. Indeed, it is rarely otherwise. Governments typically attach conditions to such payments to prevent recipients from re-lending their money in the open market and pocketing the profit, or from putting it to some other purpose not desired by government.

The *quid pro quo* for contracts can be substantive or procedural, and sometimes both. A common example of procedural conditions is the 'matching' requirement that the borrower or grantee finds a proportion of the money required for a certain project from his or her own resources or from some other source. The matching of other people's money with its own is widely used in government as a device for ensuring that the borrower or grantee has an incentive to avoid wasting money or to ensure that the project seems sensible to scrutineers from another money-providing source and is under surveillance from another quarter.

Of course, this tactic is by no means unique to government. Insurance companies work on exactly the same basis when they require us to bear a part of any loss out of our own resources, to prevent carelessness and trivial claims. So do merchant banks when they require a borrower to have a personal financial stake in a project for which he or she is seeking a loan.

Naturally, the device has its limitations. There is an obvious possibility of greater delay when such conditions are imposed, and some projects may never be undertaken if government insists on a matching formula. Even if they are undertaken, there is no absolute guarantee against waste. For example, the contributions that the British government required from local landowners when it financed road- and bridge-building in the Scottish highlands in the early nineteenth century did not prevent conspicuous waste and failure owing to the incompetence of the contractors in many cases (Haldane, 1962).

Transfers

The other main way in which government gives its treasure to particular individuals is via what may be called *transfers*. When it uses 'transfers', government is not exchanging its treasure for a direct *quid pro quo*. In that sense, transfers are 'gifts'. They are made to people with whom government wants to curry favour (such as visiting heads of state) or to whom it is pledged to make payments (such as widows or the chronic sick). Sometimes they are used for more exotic 'slush fund' purposes, as in the case of money covertly paid by governments to organisations sympathetic to their aims. A well known example is the (then) secret US government funds channelled by the CIA after the Second World War into journals favoured by policy-makers in Washington and into organisations such as the Congress of Cultural Freedom and the National Student Association (see Colby, 1978).

Transfers in this sense are not only 'unconditional'. They are also particular, in the sense that they are made one by one and that the identity of the person or organisation with which government is dealing is important. Government will not engage in these transactions with just anyone. At the least the payee will typically need a proof of identity or a signature to be checked against a specimen signature, and in some cases the payment may be very much more particular than that.

Transfers are, of course, one of the commonest instruments of government. The modern era of government money payments to millions of individuals – such as pensions and welfare benefits – makes heavy demands on government's treasure. The numbers involved typically require government to 'departicularise' the process of individual payment as far as it can, so that each transaction fits into an assembly line of similar transactions. Typically, just as banks and private firms use a variety of credit-card schemes for clients to obtain cash and goods, government equips individual payees with tokens of entitlement of a kind that will be discussed further in the next chapter (warrants, order books with tear-off slips, and so on) so that not much more than a cashier's job remains once these tokens are presented for payment.

Naturally, there is a narrow line in practice between contracts and transfers. For example, after the First World War the French brought in a scheme of family allowances to try to lift the French birth rate, which had fallen as a result of men lost in the war (Rose and Peters, 1978, p. 77). Such payments are not 'contracts' to produce children in the same sense as contracts to produce military supplies, but merely gifts as of right to those specific individuals who have produced children. But at the margin the distinction between the two types of payment becomes fuzzy, and their effects may be similar – just as payments to 'encourage' sympathetic guerilla groups may shade into the hiring of mercenaries.

Conduits

Conduits are somewhat less particularised ways of distributing treasure than the forms that have just been outlined. Conduits employ intermediaries to move treasure to its final recipient. They can be used both for exchanges and for 'unconditional' payments.

Just as we saw with group-directed methods of disseminating information in the last chapter, the use of individuals or organisations as wholesalers in the movement of money is far from uncommon as a device of government. In taxation, the principle is very old, going back to the days when governments 'farmed' taxes, using outside contractors to collect tax payments from individuals and to hand over the proceeds to government in a lump sum. In a slightly different form the conduit principle is still widely used in taxation, with government using companies and organisations as the channel for collecting income taxes, social security taxes, sales taxes and so on. Its extension to paying out government money is perhaps inevitable in the modern context of cheque-book government.

Government often finds it convenient to conduit payments in

circumstances when, for good or bad reasons, it wants to avoid getting too closely involved in the decisions of how much to pay to whom. Hence many governments choose to conduits grants to individual scientists and artists through intermediary organisations in order to avoid close entanglement in questions of scientific or artistic merit. The same principle has been applied in Britain to the making of discretionary payments to families of handicapped children, involving delicate case decisions, by an independent trust using government money (Bradshaw, 1980).

The same sometimes applies to government payments to businessmen and farmers. Governments may decide to conduit compensation payments to farmers for bad-weather losses through farmers' associations, as did the British government in Scotland after a blizzard in 1978 (Richardson and Jordan, 1979). They may decide to channel investment funds to companies through venture capitalists, as in the case of an 'Anglo–American Venture Fund' set up by the British government in 1980.

In some cases, of course, intermediaries spring up quasi-spontaneously as professional negotiators and agents, helping (at a price, of course) the lay public to get their hands on a basketful of government grants and loans, with the minimum of vexation. Although this is not quite 'wholesaling' in the same sense as the examples given above, it may come to approximate to it, and may indeed simplify the process of disbursal for government as well as the public at large.

In yet other cases, government may choose to work through intermediaries as a way of 'laundering' money payments that it wishes to conceal. For example, William Colby, a former Director of the CIA, describes how, in the CIA's operations in Italy in the 1950s, heavy use was made of secret funds channelled through intermediaries so as to conceal the source of the money from the world at large and even from the final payees themselves. As a case in point, he recalls that, during elections in 1955, 'I was authorized to fill the back seat of my Fiat with millions of lire and pass them on through my outside agent, an ostensible student' (Colby and Forbath, 1978, p. 125).

Open payments

The term *open payments* is here used to refer to those cases where government hands over its treasure without much concern about the identity of those whom it is paying. This applies, for example, when treasure is used for casual purchases (without identifying the 'contracting parties') or in those publicity stunts when money is given away in the street to randomly selected individuals.

Needless to say, governments rarely disburse their treasure in this literal form. But they do on occasion make payments that are not tailor-made to the payee. The process is in some ways like a slot-machine. One may, of course, press the buttons in such a way as to make a 'personal' selection, but the machine is designed to serve anyone who has the right coins or tokens.

Bounties

The term *bounty* is taken to denote a payment made in exchange for some direct *quid pro quo*, but which is open-ended in that the individual or organisation which is to provide that *quid pro quo* is not specified. Anyone who produces the required goods or services gets the 'bounty'. An example is the reward that government may offer to anyone who hands over a certain criminal or outlaw (in contrast to the 'contract' approach of paying a particular person to do the job).

Government can pay bounties for many different purposes: for example, to encourage activities such as killing rabbits or catching fish. Often it turns out that payments of this kind, precisely by their open-ended character, can influence the behaviour of government's subjects in ways that are not intended – a problem classically analysed in 1776 by Adam Smith (1910, vol. 2, pp. 18–20) in relation to the eighteenth-century British herring subsidies.

A more recent case of the same phenomenon can be taken from the period after the First World War, when the French government tried to support its ailing fleet of merchant sailing vessels by offering a subsidy for every mile travelled by French sailing ships. The result was the transfer of a large part of the world's merchant sailing fleet to the French flag, and the collapse of the subsidy scheme under the load. This is, of course, a story that is constantly being repeated in one form or another.

'Bearer-directed' payments

The somewhat cumbersome term *'bearer-directed' payments* must serve, in the absence of a better term, to describe the 'generalised' version of payments that do not involve an immediate *quid pro quo*, but are rather a consequence of eligibility of some kind. The bearer bond is, of course, the classic case of this kind of payment (hence the name used here) and any kind of potentially transferable right to payment can operate in a similar fashion. For example, government will automatically pay us the prize when we produce the lottery ticket with the winning number on it. 'Who we are' is not especially important in such a case. The payment might well be made by slot-machines if that were practicable.

The advantage of the bearer-directed payment is that it requires minimal discrimination on the part of government at the point of payment. Indeed, as has already been noted, many of government's welfare state payments operate like this at the point where money actually changes hands. This is done by concentrating the 'particular' part of the process on the issue of official tokens, which then serve as 'coins'. Just as anyone with the right money can operate a real slot-machine, anyone who can produce the right official token (issued elsewhere) can trigger the dispenser. The advent of token-reading machines as bank cash dispensers and for other types of 'charge' transactions is already serving to move many retail-type transactions into a no man's land between transfers and bearer-directed payments. In principle, many of government's welfare payments to individuals could be conducted on the same basis.

The tool-set in context

At the end of the last chapter, it was pointed out that the various agencies of government can differ widely in the information-disseminating tools, or mixes of those tools, that they use for their tasks. We also saw how, by mixing the tools up, a wide range of possible combinations could be produced; and how the tools could on occasion be substituted for each other and for other classes of effector. Finally, there was some exploration of possible circumstances that might serve to shift government's emphasis from one kind of tool to another. Exactly the same questions can be asked in relation to treasure, although the discussion here will be much briefer.

Comparative profiles

At the actual point where government parts with its treasure to the world outside, the process is typically concentrated into special sub-units. This follows the traditional separation of accountant and cashier in the handling of money: that is, the authorisation of payment from payment itself.

In a broader sense, though, treasure is employed as an effector in many government agencies, activities and policy fields. It is, as we have seen, a commonplace of government operations. Of course, some government agencies use treasure far more than others. Some scarcely handle treasure at all, except for wage payments to their own staff: regulatory offices are typically a case in point. On the other hand, some agencies scarcely use anything else: an example is the type of economic development agency which puts heavy emphasis on offering financial incentives to 'footloose' companies to set up shop in its bailiwick.

For the USA, Weidenbaum (1969, pp. 9–10) relates the degree of emphasis placed on treasure to different bureaucratic 'generations'. He says that old-established federal government agencies (such as the Post Office, Justice Department, Department of State) typically devote the bulk of their resources to direct operations and to their own payroll, whereas newer agencies (such as the Department of Health, Education and Welfare, the National Aeronautics and Space Agency, and the Department of Transportation) tend to concentrate on giving money away through contracts of one kind or another.

Even 'treasure-heavy' agencies, of course, seldom rely on this instrument alone, but mix it up with other kinds of effectors (with the exact recipe varying in every case). For example, the central education departments in Britain base their control over the education system on a mixture of nodality, treasure and authority (Kogan, 1971; Underwood, 1977, p. 98): organisation figures very little in their operations. Other kinds of agency mix organisation and treasure: for example, the US Army Corps of Engineers or agencies in the business of agriculture or forestry.

Moreover, those government agencies that put a heavy emphasis on 'money-moving' typically differ in the instruments that they employ for dispensing their treasure. For example, unemployment benefit offices and welfare agencies are money-moving agencies which typically place the emphasis on customised payments in the form of transfers, moving money in 'penny pieces' to individuals. Environmental agencies will typically dispense their treasure in the form of contracts of one kind or another. Other money-moving agencies, such as those involved in subsidising the arts or the sciences, may put more emphasis on conduits, moving money in larger lumps.

Combinations and substitutions

As we saw for information-dispensing in Chapter 2, government can link together its different ways of dispensing treasure, such that a large number of possible patterns may arise in combination. For example, government might seek to assist fishermen by a mixture of bounties (for every unit weight of fish caught) and contracts (loans or grants to individuals for building or improving boats). Typically it assists the unemployed by a mixture of transfers (welfare payments to individuals), contracts (grants to organisations promoting schemes for temporary employment), and perhaps also conduits (grants to 'talent-spotting' intermediaries).

Government can also *substitute* one method of dispensing treasure for another, or indeed substitute money-moving as a whole for other kinds of effectors. An example of the former is the substitution of conduits for customised payments, for example in channelling international aid payments through aid organisations rather than paying directly to the target individuals or groups.

As far as the second kind of substitution is concerned, it is almost in the nature of treasure to be substitutable for other kinds of effector, and in many 'normal' circumstances that will indeed be the case. For example, subsidies or cash incentives may be substitutable for exhortation or propaganda. The same may apply to money incentives as against orders based on authority. Government may conscript troops or recruit them on the open market, matching the financial incentives offered by other potential employers. It may offer payments to its subjects not to produce commodities that are in surplus, or simply impose production quotas. It may use authority in the form of guarantees, or tax concessions, which may do exactly the same job as actually handing out its treasure, even though no money changes hands in a literal sense, and have thus come to be known as 'tax expenditures' (Heald, 1983, ch. 2).

Similarly, treasure is substitutable for 'organisation' over a wide range of applications. The cheque-book is often a substitute for doing it yourself, for government as well as for individuals. Just as 'cheque-book journalism' means paying people in the news to reveal their stories in an exclusive way as 'confessions' and the like, instead of having journalists go to the trouble of ferreting out the relevant facts, so government can use 'cheque-book government' instead of organisation and direct action.

Military supply is one well known case of this. Before the nineteenth century, there was no military-industrial complex (in the sense of a defence 'sector' of semi-independent companies producing armaments and other supplies for the armed forces) on anything like the present scale in countries like Britain and the USA (Hood, 1976, pp. 30–1). Government made all of its own armaments and most of its military equipment, even down to items such as military uniforms. Today the bulk of these items are made by outside contractors in Britain and the USA. Government just writes the cheques.

The same applies to a large range of other activities for which government can choose between paying others to perform the task in question, or carrying it out 'in-house'. For example, government can make its money and medals by manufacturing them in its own mints, or contract such production to others (private firms, other governments). It can dredge fishery harbours itself (as it does in Scotland) or pay others to do the job. And so on, for everything from security patrols to garbage collection.

Treasure and cheque-book government: protases

Chapter 2 concluded with a discussion of the circumstances in which government is likely to have to switch its emphasis from some kinds of information-dispensers to others, and from information-dispensing as a whole to other kinds of effectors. The same pattern will be followed here, but in a much briefer and rather more tentative way. Here I shall comment on only two possible factors bearing on government's use of its cheque-book. These are the size of population with which government is dealing, and the wider social context within which government operates.

(1) *Size of population.* It was suggested in the last chapter that the more 'particular' forms of information-dispensing would typically tax government's bureaucratic resources more heavily than more 'general' types, at least when the population to be dealt with was large. The same applies to the dispensing of government's treasure. The more that government cashiers have to take account of the particular identity and circumstances of each person to whom they must hand out money, the more laborious the process will be. Certainly, if all payments to individuals had to be *totally* 'customised' – through formal presentation ceremonies or special conditions of payment – government would quickly grind to a halt.

Of course, there are some types of money payment that can never be standardised or channelled through intermediaries. But wherever the client population is large or where payment is repetitive, the bureaucracy-intensive character of totally customised forms of payment will lead government to look for means of making life easier for itself in some way. As we have seen, this often means turning transfers into a form of bearer-directed payments. Similarly, conduit payment has been used by governments for a very long time as a way of saving the bureaucratic effort involved in transacting individual payments, and it will come almost instinctively to the administrative mind in some cases. Much administrative skill in this age of cheque-book government goes into devising bureaucracy-saving conduits and standard payment systems.

(2) *The wider social context*. The great advantage of cheque-book government, as opposed to the other kinds of effectors available to government, is that it can be used to further purposes which government cannot completely specify – not merely to secure obedience or compliance, but to induce its subjects to positive or creative activity or to choose the best means of achieving some broadly specified goal. Government's other effectors may on occasion be used in this way as well, but they do not lend themselves to it so readily. In principle, treasure is an elegant effecting tool capable of being wielded with great finesse to achieve a finely balanced incentive structure.

Perhaps this is the reason for the apparently growing emphasis on cheque-book government in some countries, a phenomenon to which we will be returning in Part III. But there are, of course, limits to the extent to which government can retreat into the role of a banker, controlling society solely by its ability to offer money or to cut it off. Even in the best of circumstances, there are service and manufacturing operations that must be under government's direct control in order for it to *be* a government.

Moreover, it is in the nature of treasure – unlike nodality and authority, to which we come in the next chapter – that, once spent, it has to be replenished. Outside the world of legends and fairy stories, treasure does not renew itself; and refuelling its stores of treasure can make heavy demands on government's detecting apparatus as well as on its effectors based on authority and organisation. Treasure can therefore be a costly instrument for government to use, in contrast, say, to 'tax expenditures', unless it brings immediate money returns in forms such as interest payments. The implications of this are explored in Chapter 8.

Moreover, as government comes under pressure and encounters

increasing resistance to its regime, the more difficult it is likely to be for government to direct its treasure accurately, and the more expensive the process of replenishing its stocks of treasure is likely to be. 'Directionality' (the capacity to move treasure accurately to a specific target) is lost and immediate money returns are less likely to flow in, as payees default on debts, 'welsh' on contracts, or put government's money to purposes quite other than those officially intended. Even to be seen personally receiving government's treasure may become dangerous, so that government has to switch away from customised payments to conduits or open payments, even if that means diminished control and more unfairness.

Similarly, as the pressure mounts it may become costlier for government to renew its treasure. Growing disobedience by subjects may make loans to government dry up, except on punitive conditions, and may mean increasing resistance to taxation and its analogues. At the same time, larger money rewards may be needed to maintain loyalty and to perform important tasks, as the 'price' of compliance goes up. In circumstances such as these, the role of a mere banker becomes harder for government to sustain. Coercive force, if it is strong enough, can always be used to secure treasure; but cheque-book operations will not necessarily buy physical support.

Hence cheque-book government may have something of the character of a 'fair weather' instrument. It is likely to be a 'lead' instrument of government in a fairly consensual society, or at least in a world in which individuals are able to be highly receptive to the short-term balance of financial advantage, so that they are prepared to respond readily to the money incentives offered by government and to use the funds more or less as government intends. There is some parallel here to nodality, as explored in Chapter 2 – another resource which appears to become harder for government to lean upon as social hostility rises.

Of course, even in fairly high consensus circumstances, the payments that government offers may not achieve the desired result. Dishonesty, incompetence and malign chance will always take their toll. But treasure may be increasingly unreliable when government is *in extremis*. When it is our lives rather than our bank balances that are at stake, we may become decreasingly responsive to the cheque-book mode of government. Lasswell and Kaplan (1950, p. 93) quote Solon's telling comment on the wealth of the Croesus, which can serve as a counterpoint to the epigraph at the beginning of this chapter: 'If another king come that hath better iron than you, he will be master of all this gold'.

4 Tokens of Authority

. . . and that's official.

(popular daily phrase)

One of the four basic resources of government that were discussed in Chapter 1 was legal authority. This is the ability to command and prohibit, commend and permit, through recognised procedures and identifying symbols, for example the Great Seal, the Privy Seal, the 'sign manual' and the many other devices employed by governments to lend 'officiality' to their pronouncements.

We will not concern ourselves here with the *source* of government's authority, whether it be popular election, the Divine Right of Kings, or the many other doctrines on which governments may base their claim to rule. What is of interest here is the way in which government *uses* authority as an instrument. It 'spends' this resource in the form of what can be called *tokens of authority*.

A token of authority can be thought of, metaphorically, as a piece of paper with an official stamp on it, although in reality such tokens need not take that literal form. The term is perhaps somewhat over-portentous for the mundane reality of many of the devices that convey government's authority, which are often far removed from the *lettre de cachet* or the imperial decree. But there is no satisfactory word in English that can serve as a generic term to cover official tokens of all kinds. The German word *Schein* perhaps comes close to it.

As with government's messages and payments, its tokens of authority are ubiquitous. Orders, bans, requisitions, vouchers, warrants, coupons, licences, quotas, certificates . . . once you start looking, you see them everywhere. They are intended to convey authority, not simply information, to the outside world. Indeed, it often happens that a mere piece of paper with an official stamp or signature on it may be extremely valuable and eagerly sought after: for example, government guarantees for bank loans or operator licences for air routes or television stations. Other kinds of official token, such as requisition orders or military call-up papers, may be considerably less welcome.

In another sense, of course, the official token is 'no more' than a metaphorical piece of paper with an official stamp on it. Naturally, legal authority may not be sufficient in practice to ensure that government's official tokens are automatically obeyed or respected. Government's subjects may well decide to ignore the intendedly authoritative pieces of paper that it issues. In fact this happens quite frequently. In such circumstances, government must look to a different set of tools if it wishes to make any impression on the world outside.

Types of official tokens

As a way of indicating some of the different tokens of authority that government can wield, two basic distinctions will be made in this chapter. The first is the distinction between 'particular' and 'general' applications, which by now will be becoming familiar. Particular kinds of tokens – here called *directed tokens* – are those which relate to specific and named individuals, places, organisations or objects. Operators' licences are a case in point. By contrast, official tokens which are general – here called *blanketed tokens* – apply to anyone or everyone. Traffic lights or 'no smoking' notices are examples.

The other distinction relates to the degree of *constraint* that official tokens seek to introduce into the behaviour of government's subjects. Low-constraint tokens merely approve or recommend; high-constraint tokens order or forbid. An example of the former is the US Navy's 'E' award, which was given to factories with high production in the Second World War (Simon, Smithburg and Thompson, 1950, p. 472). An example of the latter is government's exercise of 'eminent domain' (that is, the legal power to compel the sale of land for government purposes). In between is a set of tokens, such as bargains and permits, which involve an intermediate degree of constraint.

The first part of this chapter briefly discusses some of the different kinds of official tokens available to government, beginning with low-constraint 'directed' tokens and concluding with high-constraint 'blanketed' ones. In the second part of the chapter, the contexts and combinations in which government uses official tokens will be explored.

Directed tokens

Certificates are perhaps the least constraining form of directed tokens. A 'certificate', in the sense used here, is essentially an authoritative declaration about the properties of an individual or object, often in terms of fitness or unfitness. This is necessarily 'particular' and it involves low constraint in that it need not of itself convey any privilege or sanction. It is a mixture of giving information and wielding authority.

The most straightforward kind of certificate is that which states the facts of a case in an (intendedly) authoritative way. Many organisations – not just government – use a host of stamps, cards or seals to officially identify employees, documents or other items. Examples are the detective's card, the bank teller's stamp, and even the stamps and stickers sometimes used by printing trade unions to certify that a piece of work destined for a print-shop has been carried out by members of the union. Birth certificates are an example specific to government.

Somewhat less straightforward are certificates which attest to less matter-of-fact properties. Examples are government's certification of trade unions as independent (as opposed to the 'bogus' creations of employers) or its certificates of academic or technical achievement, such as seamen's proficiency certificates.

There are at least three circumstances in which government need look no further than certification in its tool-kit to find an instrument for influencing social behaviour. First, the need for some common or approved standards may be sufficient to give government's certificates a value. For example, since 1976 government in Britain has officially certified the fuel consumption of each make of motor car, in order to provide 'authoritative' figures for consumers.

Second, and closely related, the award of government's 'seal of approval' may be prized and eagerly sought after as intrinsically desirable. Government's honours and medals are perhaps the clearest example: many of them involve little or nothing in the way of concrete privileges and so amount to little more than official certificates of merit to individuals. Similarly, companies in Britain have long valued the social *cachet* that their products can acquire as a result of displaying the 'royal warrant'; and the same principle was recently applied in a slightly different sphere, in the award of government certificates to successful export firms.

Indeed, even at very much more mundane levels, government's 'seal of approval' is often valuable to businessmen and traders, as a means of inspiring confidence among their customers. For example, many roadside petrol pumps in Britain were voluntarily submitted for testing and certification by the Board of Trade long before that process became compulsory in 1926 (Llewellyn Smith, 1928, p. 164).

Third, we may want a certificate from one government in order to get something from another government. For instance, we may need our home government's certificates of specifications or other documents if we are applying for patents from another government; we may need to get official certificates of purity in order to export livestock or animal products to another country; or if we are moving between countries with reciprocal arrangements for medical benefits, we will need a certificate of entitlement from our home government.

In such circumstances, certification may be an effective instrument for government to use, without requiring it to invoke any element of compulsion. In other cases, of course, government may be able to do *no more* than offer certificates in the hope that they will have an effect. Certification must serve *faute de mieux*. For example, government may find itself unable to guarantee work to the unemployed, but it can give such people official certificates to prove that they have been on a government training course or job-creation project. It may not be able to forbid young children to bicycle on the street without a permit, but it can encourage them to take cycling tests in order to obtain certificates of competence from the police.

Medium-constraint varieties

Certificates are 'directed tokens' involving very low constraint on the behaviour of government's subjects. Before coming to the high-constraint variety, I shall discuss an intermediate category of medium-constraint directed tokens. Within this category fall what we can call *conditional tokens* and *enablements*.

(a) *Conditional tokens*. A 'conditional' token is an undertaking (promise, threat) by government to do *x* if *y* happens. Of course, many official tokens have conditions attached to them, but in the pure case of the 'conditional', events or behaviours other than *y* are not prohibited (except, perhaps, by ordinary rules such as laws of fraud or contract). We can take government's deal or not, just as we choose. The outcome depends explicitly on the turn of events or on the behaviour of others with whom government is dealing. That is why conditionals can be considered as involving a middle level of constraint.

Government guarantees are perhaps the best example of the pure conditional. Most governments have schemes for guaranteeing approved exports against default by overseas clients, or for guaranteeing overseas investment against political risks such as revolutions or *coups d'ètat*. Governments may likewise guarantee the loans made by private banks to particular institutions. Dramatic examples from the USA are the so-called 'Lockheed loan' of $250 million in 1975 and the 'Chrysler loan' of $1,000 million in 1980. In fact, these were not loans at all as far as the US government was concerned. All that passed between the US government and these companies was an official slip of paper saying that the federal government would guarantee bank loans up to the stated amount. That was the only 'constraint' needed to prevent the firms concerned from going bankrupt, because it allowed them to borrow money on the private market on terms that would otherwise not have been available (Lowi and Stone, 1978, p. 22).

(b) *Enablements*. Conditional tokens such as bonds, guarantees and contracts may be constraining in the sense that they convey 'an offer you can't refuse', but there is no formal prohibition on 'unlicensed' activity. You are not forbidden from exporting or borrowing without government guarantees if you can do it. By contrast, an 'enablement', as it is termed here, is a token which permits you to carry on an activity which would otherwise be positively prohibited. Alternatively it may convey rights of allocation or exemption from some government rule or payment that would otherwise apply. 'Enablements' belong in the medium-constraint category because they only allow, but do not *compel*, you to undertake the activity in question.

Like certificates, enablements are a commonplace device in every organisation. Outside government we find them everywhere, in forms which range from the trivial (the parking permit, the boarding card) to the more fundamental. An example of the latter is the individual permits that were issued by trade unions during the Ulster General Strike of 1974 to allow particular individuals to work, to buy petrol or to pass through the barricades that were erected in the streets.

For government itself, enablements are a long-established instrument. Governments have always been in the business of issuing licences, charters and letters patent granting privileges of a variety of kinds. Old-time examples include licences for traffic, for markets and fairs, and censoring the news media. It may use more direct methods, such as physically seizing or destroying dangerous information by exposing film and burning or shredding books or papers. It may simply shut down its own detectors. Hence government may alter or abandon some types of statistical collection if the information relayed by such detectors turns out to be consistently bad news for government. For example, the French government destroyed its own electoral register for Ploermel in 1873 in order to postpone a difficult election (Machin, 1977, p. 23).

We will come to applications such as these later. For now we shall concentrate on information put out directly by government.

Bespoke messages

The most 'particular' form of information that government dispenses can be called '*bespoke messages*', because the information is individually tailored to each informee.

There are at least three main ways in which government can convey a 'bespoke message'. The first is to provide replies tailored to unsolicited questions. We could call this an *unprompted query response*. Government gives information out in this way when it cannot predict accurately what may be demanded. Most government agencies have general-purpose inquiry points to handle – or head off – awkward questions that may come out of the blue. Alternatively government may use this device when it has information which for one reason or another it does not wish to propagate, without invoking formal secrecy. By 'waiting to be asked' – thereby throwing all the onus on to the would-be informee – and by acting with computer-like literalness, thus volunteering information only when exactly the right question is asked, government may make the acquisition of official information by outsiders all but impossible without a high degree of pertinacity, expertise or luck.

A second method of conveying a bespoke message is similar, in that it involves a reply tailored to each individual inquiry. The difference is that in this case the question does not quite come out of the blue. Government actually *invites* its subjects to seek enlightenment, by advertising the information which it has available.

We could call this a *prompted query response*. The 'response' may on occasion be access to raw information rather than the provision of processed information: for example, when government allows us to search for entries in one of its many registers or repositories. The message targets (Knightley, 1975). Indeed, it commonly happens that the more information that government wishes to suppress, the more carefully it will have to try to structure what is available. Camouflage – both in its military and looser colloquial sense – often entails a laborious task of putting out misleading information.

Government propagation and suppression of information is linked in other ways, too. For example, the more information that government labels as officially secret, the more widespread is likely to be the unofficial 'leakage' of information from the government's bureaucracy by 'moles'. Indeed, just as a pig may sometimes be made to go forward by pulling it backwards by the tail, so government may give information greater drama and currency by apparently trying to keep it secret. In this way, government disseminates information by appearing to suppress it. Suppression and propagation of information can often be opposite sides of the same coin.

Direct information propagation

This chapter is about the information government puts out *itself*. It is in two main sections. The first section is a broad outline of devices available to government for putting out information. The discussion begins with the most 'particular' devices – those cases where government tailors its message to each individual informee – and ends with the most 'general', where the message is directed to the world at large or to whomever it may concern. The second section of the chapter discusses the contexts in which different kinds of information-dispenser may be used, and the way in which the various types get mixed up in action.

Of course, there are many ways in which governments may propagate information other than by putting it out themselves. Government can do the job by using the tools discussed in the next few chapters. It can pay others to promote some cause or to give out information, using its cheque-book as the chosen instrument. Or it can *require* others to propagate certain types of information, as happens with the regulations which it lays down for food labelling, bankrupt and limited-liability companies, or health warnings on cigarette packs.

Similarly, when government wants to suppress information, there are other ways of doing the job than putting out its own messages. Government may use its legal authority to permit and forbid, for example in 'patents' in the modern sense of licences granting a temporary monopoly to inventors. Sometimes such enablements conveyed coercive powers, such as letters of marque (licences to commit piracy on foreign merchant ships) or the powers obtained by the London Fishmongers' Company in the seventeenth century to enter and search shops and to seize and dispose of any fish found to be bad.

Today, government enablements cover a bewildering range of activity. For example, if you want to run a zoo, an employment agency, a casino, an abattoir, an animal experiment laboratory, a pharmacy or a data bank on individuals indicating their creditworthiness, you will need permission from a central government agency in Britain. The list is endless, running from putting up a garage in your garden to discharging nuclear waste or burning heather and grass on your grouse moor, should you happen to own one. Nor, apparently, is there any escape in fiction: even Ian Fleming's famous secret agent '007' had to be 'licensed to kill'.

Enablements are 'everywhere' partly because, like certificates, they are one of the most basic tools used to regulate business. Government may require you to be licensed for a certain *activity* – when you are importing or exporting food, say, or armaments on government's 'strategic goods list'. It may require you to be licensed to trade over a *period*, as in the case of taxi-cabs. It may require you to ask its permission to *change* your activities or standards of service. Arguments constantly go on as to whether government should use licensing to regulate this or that trade or activity: sex shops, private security firms, marriage bureaux, citizens' band radio operators, or whatever the current political argument is about.

Enablements go under many different names in practice, such as licences, warrants, quotas, coupons, vouchers, permits, exemption certificates. The differences in terminology are often misleading. But there are real differences in the way government can go about giving enablements. For example, they can be limited or unlimited, qualitative or quantitative. A brief comment will be made on each of these types.

First, the difference between limited and unlimited enablements. Sometimes official permissions to carry on an activity are issued in restricted quantities rather than without limit to anyone who qualifies (such as drivers' licences). Examples of the former are casino licences, work permits or immigrant admission vouchers. Limiting enablements to a fixed number may sometimes make them valuable and so give an incentive to permit-holders to police their privileges themselves, for example by informing on illegal activity or 'cowboy' operators.

Second, the difference between qualitative and quantitative enablements. Most of the examples that have been discussed so far are discrete or qualitative, like a safe-conduct (either you get the token or you don't). But some government enablements are quantitative. They specify a quota or a point along a scale. A common example is the production quota, which allows a particular undertaking to do so much and no more. These are widely used in controlling farm produce, fishermen's catches, even land development, in those cases where official permission to develop is accompanied by a limit on the size of building that can be erected on any particular site (so-called 'plot ratios').

Most of the examples of enablements given here have been in the realm of business regulation. Of course, the device is used in many other contexts: for instance, the tokens which grant parole or bail to prisoners, or the tokens which entitle individuals to obtain money, goods or services from government or from some other source. Ration cards or old-age pension order books are examples of the latter; and the development of the modern 'welfare state' has been accompanied, as we saw in Chapter 3, by the heavy use of enablements of this kind.

Constraints

The term *constraints* stands, in a self-explanatory way, for the most constraining form of directed token. Constraints, in contrast to certificates, conditionals and enablements, positively demand or prohibit an activity.

Constraints can be negative or positive, sometimes both at the same time. Negative constraints are prohibitions laid on particular individuals or items. A well known example is the 'cease and desist' order which the US Federal Trade Commission can apply to firms engaged in trade practices deemed to be 'unfair'. Similarly, between 1947 and 1958, British government agriculture committees issued orders dispossessing 400 farmers and landowners whose land was deemed by government inspectors to be unsatisfactorily farmed (Self and Storing, 1962, p. 111).

The other side of the coin is the order that requires positive action. Government may call us up for military service or requisition our property. It may order the slaughter of diseased livestock or the felling of trees affected by pests. It may require the repair, demolition, sale or evacuation of specific buildings. It may issue compulsory cropping orders to raise the output of agricultural land, as happened in Britain in the

Second World War. It may billet troops or evacuees in civilian households.

Indeed, government may sometimes choose to combine prohibitions and positive injunctions in a double-barrelled operation. In Britain, for example, government may both order the broadcasting authorities to desist from transmitting specified material *and* require certain material of its own to be broadcast by them.

An important variation on the theme is what may be called an 'arbitrament'. In this case, government uses its official authority to constrain against a background of conflict – or at least of potential conflict – between two or more parties. It sets itself up as an appeal court against the actions of other individuals, agencies or organizations.

Arbitraments are a long-standing type of constraint, going back to royal involvement in quarrels between powerful barons. When the royal bureaucracy had grown larger, the device was in turn taken up by the King's servants, and it is still used quite widely today. For example, government arbitration in labour disputes was compulsory in Britain during the Second World War, when strikes were officially prohibited; and compulsory arbitration by government in some kinds of labour disputes has from time to time been favoured as a tool of policy by would-be reformers in the post-1945 period, notably in the ill-fated proposals for industrial relations legislation formulated by the Labour government in 1968–9.

Group-targeted tokens

The kinds of official tokens that have been discussed so far are all 'particular', in the sense that they apply to specific individuals, organisations or items. In the next section I shall look at more general types; but before passing on to that it is worth noting very briefly that government sometimes chooses a half-way house between general and particular, using the medium of *groups* – just as applies to its other kinds of effecting tools.

For example, government often conduits its certificates and enablements through organised groups. Jewish traders in Britain may be exempted from the laws restricting trading on Sundays, but the certification of such traders as *bona fide* Jews is done by the Jewish Board of Deputies, not by government (Alderman, 1982, pp. 99–104). Another case is the certification of motor vehicles as roadworthy, which in several countries is done by (licensed) private garages rather than by government officials in person.

It is rarer to find group-directed applications of constraints in a strict sense (in 'liberal' regimes, at least), but group-directed applications of conditional tokens are by no means uncommon. British governments in the 1970s repeatedly tried to apply them to the labour union 'peak' association (the Trades Union Congress), offering pro-labour measures in exchange for pay restraint or threatening to raise taxes in the event of union pay increases exceeding a certain level.

Blanketed tokens

Blanketed tokens are official tokens that are 'general', applying to the world at large or to whomever it may concern. Each of the 'targeted' types of token discussed earlier can be translated into a general or 'blanketed' form. A very brief discussion of this must suffice.

Certification in its general form can be termed *standard approval*. This denotes those tokens used by government to lend its authority to certify or approve, but without necessarily implying constraint or entitlement. There are two ways in which certification can be 'generalised'. One, the weaker sense, is to make certificates transferable, as applies in those cases where a certificate may be transferred on a change of ownership.

The other way is for government to approve or lay down targets or codes of good behaviour – standards which are not legally binding but are self-consciously 'official'. An example is 'government time', the official measurement of time and its accompanying conventions such as putting clocks back and forward in autumn and spring in order to save daylight. No one forces us to use 'government time' in our own private affairs, but most of us do. Similarly, government may choose to issue codes of good conduct in matters such as driving behaviour or labour–management relations – codes which are not legally binding but which bear a heavy stamp of official approval (perhaps suitable for production as evidence in court). This kind of standard-setting takes us on to the interesting borderline territory between the token of official authority and the information-dispenser.

Open compacts

The general form of the 'conditional' token may be termed an *open compact*. This is used by government to offer a bargain, not to specific individuals or groups, but to whomever the matter may concern.

A well known example is the amnesty, a device that is used commonly enough for tax defaulters, for the illegal possession of weapons, and even for overdue library books. Governments guarantees that it will not try to punish anyone who declares past misdemeanours or hands in proscribed items. But amnesties are usually linked with threats of heavy penalties against future offenders, of course.

Indeed, the promise 'to pay the bearer on demand', quaintly preserved on British paper money, is a relic of an 'open compact', although it is an obsolete and empty one, as anyone who presents banknotes to one of the note-issuing banks can discover.

Open permits

Enablements in their general form might be termed *open permits*. Enablements, like certificates, can become generalised if they are transferable; and indeed many enablements that are particular in the sense that they apply to a named object, organisation or animal, may also be 'general' in the sense that they are transferable among people. Entitlement is then a matter of the document or of the number of government vouchers that you can produce, not by 'who you are'. Private-sector equivalents are trading stamps, 'packet-top' offers and the like.

Examples of open permits may include vehicle licences, taxi plates or decals and permits for land development. Even production quotas can sometimes take this form. For example, in the late 1920s any farmer who wished to start growing hops in Britain could only do so by buying the necessary tokens from other farmers who already held hop quotas (Self and Storing, 1962, p. 89). On occasion a lively market can develop in open permits.

Another application of open permits is to sanction activity which government normally forbids: for example, if government lifts its normal evening curfew for everyone on the occasion of a holiday or relaxes city car parking restrictions during a train strike.

Standard constraints

Constraints in their general form might be termed *standard constraints*. Standard constraints are those compulsory edicts of government that apply to the world at large, or to whomever it may concern.

Like their 'directed' equivalents, standard constraints can be negative or positive. Examples of the negative variety are not hard to find. Governments often issue general prohibitions of certain products or activities, as did the EEC when it banned the import of leather treated with whale oil in 1982. Water authorities may forbid the use of garden hosepipes in times of drought. Fishing agencies may ban certain types of fishing or fishing equipment. Agricultural agencies may ban livestock movement in order to prevent the spread of animal disease. No named individual, of course, is involved in such prohibitions.

Equally common are standard constraints from government which require action of a more positive kind. Government often sets standards, not in the non-mandatory 'standard approval' form, but by demanding that the standards be observed by anyone who wishes to undertake a certain activity. We may not be obliged to observe 'government time', but we are obliged to observe government's speed limits. Government may demand that all petrol be stored in metal containers. It may demand that all houses be built of brick or stone. It may set minimum or maximum prices at which goods may be sold.

An interesting application of standard constraints, touched upon in Chapter 2, is the requirement sometimes laid by government on those whom it may concern to transmit a message to the public, as a way of saving government from having to do the job itself. An example from the 1850s is the government requirement that limited-liability companies add a word to their names (e.g. 'Inc.', 'Ltd', 'PLC', 'AG') to signify this. This was an administrative invention which Llewellyn Smith (1928, pp. 165–6) regarded as a master-stroke, since it conveyed a public warning at no cost to the government.

Since the nineteenth century, this application of standard constraints has been greatly extended, becoming almost a commonplace of government administration today. If we are learning to drive, we may be required to signify the fact to other road users. If we are an undischarged bankrupt, we may be required to signify the fact when obtaining credit. Tobacco companies may be required to display government health warnings on cigarette packs and advertisements. Food manufacturers may be required to display details of their products on the label.

2 Advice, Information, Persuasion

'But . . . ', I attempted to explain, ' . . . that's just phony. It's dishonest, it's juggling with figures, it's pulling the wool over people's eyes.'
'A government press release, in fact', said Humphrey.

(Lynn and Jay, 1981, p. 74)

One of the four basic resources of government discussed in the last chapter was 'nodality', that is, the property of being in the middle of a social network. One of the important things that government gets from its central position is a store of information or a panoramic picture. This gives it a reason to be listened to, quite apart from any of its other government-like properties, unless it forfeits all credibility. Governments can therefore use information (or 'disinformation') as an 'effecting' tool, and have done so since ancient times.

This tool is used so extensively by modern government that in the course of a lifetime almost everyone will find that they need to obtain and understand a multitude of official leaflets and handouts. They will find themselves exposed to a wide range of government propaganda issuing from almost every conceivable communications medium, from the recruiting poster which urges youths to fight for King and country to the official lavatory paper bearing the stern injunction 'NOW WASH YOUR HANDS'. They may find themselves attending government exhibitions, consulting government registers, seeking government's advice. On occasion, without any solicitation on their part, they may receive personal messages from government: for example, if the authorities intend to demolish their house or if they have won a prize in a government lottery.

Even outside what are conventionally thought of as media of communication, we are exposed to a variety of messages from government, sometimes without being aware of it. Government frequently seeks to emphasise its own dignity or majesty by the appurtenances of 'awesome magnificence' (Sennett, 1977, Lasswell and Fox, 1979, p. 40), as in the stage management of pomp, ceremonies, regalia, architectural massiveness, ornateness and formality, paraded displays of military might, and so on. Its law courts borrow much of the apparatus of costume drama, employing clothes, buildings and other stage props designed to overawe the uninitiated: courtroom formalities, the presence of legal dignitaries in elaborate wigs and robes, or of military officers in full dress uniform, as in the case of a court-martial.

Suppression of information

Of course, all too frequently it is what government *does not* tell us that really counts. Secrecy is as important as dissemination in government's use of information, and there are almost as many ways of keeping a piece of information secret as there are of broadcasting it.

The most obvious way is merely to keep silent. For example, when there is a bad grain harvest in the USSR, as happened in 1981, the Soviet government may simply decide to leave the relevant figures out of its economic statistics. And quite apart from pervasive secretiveness about their own affairs (Rowat, 1979), governments often forbid their subjects to propagate certain information – notably material which government chooses to label as seditious, pornographic, heretical or blasphemous.

Another way of suppressing information is by propagating it. Government may 'edit' the facts, presenting information with a selective emphasis that is designed to mislead. For example, government may choose to endow its own offices or agencies with names that serve to conceal their real purpose or activity. A notorious case was the so-called State Research Bureau which operated in Uganda during the Idi Amin dictatorship of the 1970s. In reality, its 'research' consisted of tracking down and murdering people who were opposed to the government. Government offices in some cases change their names quite frequently in order to confuse their enemies or to give an appearance of rejuvenation or of a change in direction.

A third way for government to suppress information is by blatant 'disinformation', as commonly happens in wartime. To take only one well known example, the British government in the Second World War repeatedly claimed that only military targets were being bombed in Germany, at a time when it was in fact Cabinet policy to bomb civilian

elements in Table I.1 and unpack this simple tool-kit further into sub-types. You should look at Table I.1 now in order to get an idea of the ground that will be covered, but it may be more useful later on when the names have been explained a little further: it can then be used as a summary or to follow the discussion in the chapters which follow.

Advertisers of medicines may be required to include a 'data sheet' giving factual information about their medicines. It costs government little to slap standard constraints of this type on to anything it chooses, since the compliance costs are in large part met by others. (For an interesting study of 'compliance costs' imposed by the US government on business corporations, see Gatti, 1981, pp. 95–129.)

The tool-set in context

The catalogue set out here is only a rough and ready one, intended to show some of the broadly different ways in which government can deploy its 'authority' as an instrument. There are, of course, cases that do not fit neatly into one category or another. For example, is a passport to be interpreted as a certificate (of identity and nationality) or might it really be counted as an enablement? Strictly, only a visa might be held to amount to an enablement to enter or leave a specific country, where that is otherwise forbidden. But in practice international travel without passports is difficult even where it is not forbidden, and some governments (such as that of the USSR) require passports to be used for internal travel. Or again, some purists might interpret a passport as a standard constraint – an order to let the bearer pass 'without let or hindrance', as the British passport 'requests and requires' of those whom it may concern.

Leaving the inevitable difficult cases aside, however, the final part of this chapter follows the pattern of the previous two in attempting to set government's tokens of authority into context.

Comparative profiles

It should be becoming clear that there are differences in the use of the various tokens of authority that have been described here if we look across the range of government agencies and fields of policy. Some government agencies are in effect single-token organisations, concentrating on just one type. For instance, government may have an agency specialising in arbitrating labour disputes; or it may have an agency that deals only with export credit guarantees. Most governments have patent offices limiting themselves to a specialised form of enablements. On the other hand, many government agencies – notably the larger, broad-purpose agencies – will use most if not all of the kinds of official tokens described here, with the exact profile varying from case to case.

Exactly the same applies to different fields of policy. In some policy areas, we may observe the whole gamut of official tokens (or almost all of it) in use. The control of building works is a case in point. Here we find government certification relating to soundness of construction. We find enablements in the form of permissions to build and develop. We find constraints, both in the sense of orders and prohibitions (for example, orders to evacuate buildings condemned as dangerous by government officials) and also perhaps in the sense of arbitraments (such as the British government's 'call-in' system for disputed local planning decisions).

The regulation of trade is perhaps even more of a multi-token operation, encompassing virtually all of the types that have been described in this chapter, from the certification of designs and trade marks to the 'anti-dumping' order, and including licences, export guarantees and arbitraments in cases of insolvency or disputes among shareholders. On the other hand, tasks like the administration of agricultural subsidies can rest on a rather narrower base, involving a combination of certificates (of carcass weight or quality) and enablements, such as production quotas and export or import licences. As was indicated earlier, it is a rare field of policy that does not involve the use of enablements, although constraints are perhaps not in quite such general use, tending to predominate in the spheres of agriculture and trade.

Combinations, linkages and substitutions

A second point that will be clear by now is that even a small set of basic instruments can produce a very large number of combinations. Like its other 'effecting' tools, government's tokens of authority are commonly used in combination, not in isolation. They can be 'coupled up' in at least three ways.

One way is to combine official tokens in a simultaneous compound. For example, official permission to carry on some activity commonly derives, not from a single token, but from the combination of several different official tokens, all of which must be held at the same time. To operate a passenger vehicle, vessel or aircraft, government may require us to have an up-to-date certificate of air/sea/roadworthiness, to possess a licence to operate over that particular route, and to employ operatives

I HOW GOVERNMENT ACTS UPON THE WORLD: EFFECTING TOOLS

This part of the book concentrates on government's effecting tools. In Chapter 1, four basic types of effectors were outlined, based on the 'NATO scheme' (see Figure 1.2). The four chapters which follow explore each of those types.

The four basic kinds of effector can each be used by government in a *particular* or *general* way. This is a thread that will run through the entire discussion of effecting tools. *Particular* applications are those that are directed at specific and named individuals, organisations or items: for example, when government issues permits to individuals whom it has 'vetted' for some purpose. *General* applications are those that are beamed at the world at large and thus apply to whomever it may concern: for example, when government issues some prohibition or order that applies to everyone or anyone. In between the 'particular' and the 'general' come a variety of 'group' applications.

This is only a rough distinction, and even the four basic 'NATO' types are by no means totally independent of one another, overlapping somewhat at the margin. But it gives us a workable basis from which to begin. By crossing the 'particular–group–general' distinction with the four elements of the 'NATO' scheme, we find twelve basic kinds of effectors – three for each 'NATO' resource. These are shown in Table I.1 overleaf.

The chapters in this part of the book explain and discuss the twelve

TABLE I.1 Government effectors

Basic resource	NODALITY (Chapter 2)	TREASURE (Chapter 3)	AUTHORITY (Chapter 4)	ORGANISATION (Chapter 5)
'Coin' (how government 'spends' or uses the resource)	Messages	Moneys	Official tokens	Treatments
Level of application:				
Particular	Bespoke messages	Customised payments	Directed tokens	Individual treatments
Group	← Group-targeted and 'conduited' applications →			
General	Broadcast messages	Open payments	Blanketed tokens	At-large treatments

who have the specific qualifications required. Only when these tokens are added together is the permission obtained.

Another way is to make the combination sequential rather than simultaneous, with government requiring one token to be produced before it will grant the next one. For instance, government commonly requires a certificate to be produced before it will grant an enablement. Thus you may have to produce your birth certificate before government will give you a passport. Frequently the chain is longer than this (cf. Simon, Smithburg and Thompson, 1950, p. 472).

Third, just as tokens of government's authority may be linked with one another, they are everywhere linked with the other main types of government instrument discussed in this book. They 'key in' to the movement of money and physical operations by government. They are frequently linked up with government's information-dispensers and detectors. For example, government amnesties are often linked to large-scale propaganda campaigns. A different kind of example is the official procedure for winding up a dead person's estate: before you can legally do this, you need an enablement from government in the form of a certificate of probate, and applications for such certificates automatically alert government's tax-collection detectors to examine the estate.

It has been noted already in several places that government's instruments can sometimes be substituted for one another as well as combined; and the point applies to official tokens just as much as to government's other main types of instruments. For instance, standard approvals and standard constraints may often be substitutable to some extent. The same applies to certificates and enablements; and government may also have a degree of choice among directed, group or blanketed tokens in order to do a job. For example, if government wishes to restrict exports or imports, it might impose a general ban on certain types of products, or alternatively it might issue import licences or quotas (which themselves could be made either transferable or non-transferable).

Again, there may on occasion be scope for substitution or trading-off between government's tokens of authority as a group and other kinds of government instruments. As we have seen, government can choose between using its own information-dispensers and using tokens of official authority to require others to put its message across. Similarly, there are often possibilities for substitution between tokens of authority and physical operations. Government may regulate business by a set of certificates, enablements and requirements; or it may decide to set up in business on its own account. It may forbid trespassing, or employ physical devices (walls, ditches, barbed wire) which make trespassing impossible. It may approach labour–management disputes by information-dispensing, i.e. 'counselling' to find common ground between the parties, or by arbitraments which impose a binding solution.

Simon, Smithburg and Thompson (1950, p. 11) present a dramatic example of government using official tokens instead of other instruments. Inconvenienced by coal miners' strikes during the Second World War, the US government could have responded with a number of instruments, for example information or propaganda, money incentives, coercion or physical operation of the mines by government. Instead, it chose tokens of authority: an official 'seizure' of the mine. All that this seizure meant in practice was a formal declaration and an American flag flying over each mine. But this pure exercise of authority, mixed a little with a 'broadcast' message, was sufficient to end the strike.

Tokens of authority: protases

Finally, what factors may prompt government to use certain kinds of official tokens rather than others? Only two elements will be considered here, both of which have been used earlier. These are the size of the population involved and the wider social context, in the sense of the degree of overall consensus or acceptance with which government operates.

(1) *Size of population.* As we have seen with other kinds of government effector, some forms of official token are likely to be more 'expensive' for government to use than others. The greater the particularity of any token, the more discriminately can government wield its authority; but at the same time the greater is the bureaucratic input involved. Rationing schemes that involve the allocation of individual vouchers or coupons, for example, are notorious for the manpower and effort they require on the part of government. Breyer (1982, p. 267) makes the same point in the context of business regulation.

Hence, when the population involved is large, a government interested in limiting the load on its bureaucratic system must use directed tokens sparingly. It may find itself having to balance the control advantages of directed tokens against the bureaucratic costs involved. Sometimes government may be able to lighten the load by decreasing the frequency with which directed tokens have to be renewed. For example, some years ago the Federal German government extended the renewal interval of its identity cards, and the British government changed from a system of driver licences that had to be renewed every few years to a form of licence which remains in force until the driver in question reaches the age of 70, unless he or she is disqualified or suspended by a law court.

Apart from this, the only way to lighten the load is to move away from directed tokens altogether. Government can do this by switching to group-directed or blanketed tokens. For example, in the USA general rules are laid down by government for income tax liability: individuals determine their own tax liability, and the government limits itself to a checking-up role. On the other hand, in Britain individuals are obliged only to supply information about their finances to government: government then has to transform that information into a directed token in the form of an individual tax assessment signifying the sum for which each taxpayer is liable. Needless to say, the British income tax bureaucracy is very large, groans under the weight of this process, and there is recurring talk of changing over to a US-style system.

Given the continual pressure on government to apply its tokens of authority to ever-new contexts, government must rely in large part on general standards and 'codes of conduct' agreed with groups, if it is not to be swamped by issuing avalanches of individual licences, certificates, orders, prohibitions, and so on.

Of course, there are occasions on which governments may prefer blanketed to directed tokens for reasons quite other than that of economy. Sometimes the attraction of blanketed tokens lies precisely in the fact that they afford less discriminatory control while giving the appearance of government activity and concern. For example, as part of an EEC system of economic sanctions against Iran in 1980, the British government banned any 'new' contracts for British exports to Iran, except under licence. But exporters *themselves* were invited to determine what constituted 'existing' trade contracts with Iran, which were therefore not subject to the general ban. This was described as an 'honesty' system, although 'dishonesty' might be closer to the mark, as so often applies to trade sanction regimes agreed in international conclaves.

(2) *The wider social context.* What is likely to be the effect of the overall degree of consensus, or satisfaction with government on the part of its subjects, on the use of official tokens by government? In general, it may be supposed that as consensus falls, government may find itself

moving from certification through conditional tokens and enablements to constraints.

When government is widely respected and accepted, the mere lending of its name to some individual, item or activity in the form of certification or standard approval may well be all that is needed to influence its subjects. In such circumstances, it might well be wasteful and unnecessary to use other types of tokens. Where consensus is very low, however, government certificates and declarations may not merely decline in their efficacy; they may come to have a negative value, being seen as badges of shame rather than of glory. A very mild case of this occurred in the United Kingdom in 1966, when the government chose to bestow medals on the members of a then controversial pop group (the Beatles), causing a number of traditionally minded individuals to send their medals back to the government in disgust.

Even conditionals and enablements may start to falter at some point of low consensus. The power of conditionals will wane as the promises and threats of a government perceived to be shaky or untrustworthy decline in authority. Offers from government may become increasingly refusable. Its amnesties may be ignored. Even its currency, as a general guarantee of exchange value, depends for its operation on a climate of general confidence in government. When foreign currency becomes the chief medium of exchange in a country – as was the case in Scotland before the 1707 Treaty of Union with England – something has gone very wrong with this type of token.

As consensus declines, government's enablements are also likely to come under pressure, in terms of difficulties of enforcing the prohibition on those without enablements. The limited-edition type of licence or franchise system (such as applies to oil drilling sites or broadcasting channels) may come to look attractive to a government under pressure, since the device is to some degree self-policing. But even if that continues to apply *in extremis* (which is unlikely), a government which puts too much weight on this device may lose control over what is being done in its name.

Hence, as consensus declines, government has to put increasing weight on its most 'constraining' applications of authority, namely orders and prohibitions. The situation may start to approximate to that described in the grim joke about liberty under Italian Fascism: 'everything that isn't forbidden is compulsory' (Larsen, 1980, p. 54). There is perhaps a parallel with a hard-pressed superordinate who finds him- or herself finally obliged to tell a rebellious subordinate to 'do *x*, and that's an order'. But it is precisely at that point that the superordinate's authority is really 'on the line'. If the order is not respected, what happens next?

Clearly there is more than one possibility, as everyone whose orders to a child have at some time been ignored will at once realise. One thing that *may* happen is that at that point the difference between constraints and conditionals or open compacts starts to disappear. If our order has failed to have any effect, we may switch to bargaining, to the extent that we are left with any authority at all. If government orders a rebellious crowd to disperse (for example, by reading the Riot Act) and nothing happens, it may offer an amnesty instead. It may try to do deals with influential groups. But at the point when orders are merely a prelude to bargaining, government may be on very thin ice. Its tokens are becoming 'tokens of no authority'.

Alternatively, of course, the flouting of a constraint may cause government to switch away from 'authority' in any form to other kinds of effecting tools, such as information and persuasion or physical action.

Conclusion

Government's tokens of authority are ubiquitous, appearing in everything from tax collection to farm subsidies, and constantly being applied to new contexts, as some of the examples in this chapter have shown. At least in their 'constraining' form, they reveal government at its most government-like, deploying its rather special resources of legal or official authority.

But the concluding discussion of the decline in the standing of a government *in extremis* reverts to the point made at the beginning of this chapter: that government's tokens are 'no more' than self-proclaimedly authoritative pieces of paper or statements. If obedience or compliance is not automatic or readily forthcoming, the difference between betokening authority and dispensing information starts to disappear. Government's tokens are just so many pieces of paper. You might as well paper your walls with them. Some people did just that with the German banknotes that were produced by the Weimar government in the hyperinflation of the 1920s. To make its official tokens 'stick', government may have to use other kinds of effecting tools. Ultimately, it will have to turn to 'direct action' tools, which are discussed in the next chapter.

5 Organisation, Direct Action, Treatment

> **we found in one small area around Aldershot alone civil servants operating a gravel-pit, a saw-mill, a sign-writing centre, a foundry, joinery and woodworking shops, a machinery maintenance workshop and a printing business. Elsewhere there were nurseries producing shrubs and trees, installations supplying domestic water, treating sewage, sweeping roads and similar activities.**
>
> (Chapman, 1978, p. 51)

Government uses nodality, treasure and authority as the mainstay of many of its activities. But these are not, of course, the only resources available to it for effecting purposes. There is another shot in the locker. The final resource of government that was considered in Chapter 1 is 'organisation' – a label for a stock of land, buildings and equipment, and a collection of individuals with whatever skills they may have, in government's direct possession. 'Organisation' betokens capacity and capability – armies in government's own service instead of mercenaries.

For some people, 'organisation' in this sense might be held to be a compound or derivative of nodality, treasure and authority: a sub-set rather than an element of the same set. But it is treated here as at bottom a quite separate resource from the other three. It is perfectly possible to derive nodality, treasure and authority from organisation rather than the other way round. Indeed, many governments come into being through precisely that process. 'Money can be used to get men and men to get money' is an ancient dictum.

For that reason alone, we might expect government to maintain organisation in some quantity. The US federal government, for example, is an employer and landowner on a substantial scale. It has over four million bureaucrats and military personnel under its direct command

and is master of nearly 800 million acres of land (*Congressional Quarterly Weekly Report*, 1981, p. 1899).

Organisation enables government to act directly on its subjects, their property or their environment. In that sense, it is the 'business end' of government. It is the seat of government's 'defining' (Rose, 1976) or 'last resort' activities – suppression of rebellion and resistance to enemy attacks – as well as of a great variety of miscellaneous activities.

Government 'spends' organisation in *direct action* or *treatment*, and 'treatments' are commonplace instruments in its repertoire. Government may forcibly arrest us, throw us into goal, execute and bury us. It may collect, manufacture, treat, distribute, provide. The epigraph to this chapter gives only a tiny flavour of the variety of applications to which organisation may be put, and it is impossible to do more than expand that sketch a little within the compass of a short chapter.

This chapter has the same format as the last. The first part gives some indication of the range of 'treatments' that can be applied by government, beginning with treatments that are particular and working through to more general ones. The second part comments briefly on ways in which treatments are put to use, linkages and substitutions, and explores some of the circumstances in which government applies treatment in different forms.

Individual treatment

Individual treatment is used to refer to all those cases where government acts directly on the persons or property of specific individuals or organisations. Treatment comes in at least four main forms: It may consist of *marking* an item, for example in marking the houses of victims during a plague; it may consist of *storage*, as in the case of government bonded stores; it may consist of *moving* or *distributing* some item in a physical sense, for example when government transports convicts or refugees; or it may consist of *processing* an item, changing its state, as government does when it vaccinates beasts against animal diseases. Each of these applications will be discussed briefly.

Marking

Marking is (usually, at least) a mild and almost necessarily particular form of treatment. It has a range of applications, many of them, 'humdrum'. Government may colour alcohol or oil fuels to show that tax has been paid, just as in former times it put seals on rolls of imported tobacco that had been through customs. Much the same principle is commonly used in agricultural subsidisation, when government marks animals as a means of preventing them from being presented for subsidy twice over, for example by punching the ears of subsidised claves. Older people in Britain will remember the system of government marking of eggs between 1957 and 1968 (Giddings, 1974, p. 201), which was also a means of preventing the subsidy from being paid on the same egg twice over.

Other applications of marking do not quite have this everyday character. For example, government sometimes marks the very persons of its subjects, for instance when it brands them as a form of punishment or when (as in some African or Latin American countries) it physically marks voters with indelible dye after they have cast their ballots, in order to prevent multiple voting. Such cases of marking are, of course, comparatively rare. Government tends to 'mark' people in less direct ways, either by using its authority to require its subjects to signify the characteristics in question, or by issuing them with special clothes, identity cards or discs.

Storage and custody

Storage and custody is another form of treatment which has a range of applications from the mild or everyday kind to more coercive or repressive uses.

The former type is manifested in the many cases when government offers custodial or storage facilities on a voluntary basis to particular individuals. For example, government in many countries is a banker on a large scale, offering custody of our money. The National Girobank in the United Kingdom has millions of individual accounts. Government may even offer its services as a manager of our investments, as does the British Public Trustee Office (this is an Edwardian relic, created in 1906, in the days when married women could not legally own property except through trusts; it still handles investments in about 6,000 trusts).

Sometimes the storage or custody that government offers is of a more physical nature. For example, government may maintain animal quarantine stations as a means of helping livestock exporters to meet the quarantine requirements of overseas governments. Government may provide voluntary custodianship over individuals, such as refugee camps or hostels for the homeless.

Frequently, of course, government storage or custody is not offered for us to take up or not as we wish, but is compulsorily imposed upon us. For example, compulsory storage is a traditional method used by government in the United Kingdom for enforcing excise taxes; government also keeps the keys for methylators in order to control the 'denaturing' of spirits, and maintains bonded stores for untaxed products, on which duty must be paid as the product leaves the store.

Government applies this form of treatment somewhat more coercively when it is the persons rather than the property of its subjects that are compulsorily detained. Governments operate prisons, borstals, remand centres, detention centres, juvenile correctional institutions and mental hospitals for those defined as criminally insane. They may choose to set up internment camps for imprisoning those perceived as potential dissidents or threats to the regime, as did the US government to Japanese Americans during the Second World War and the British government in Northern Ireland from 1971 to 1975, using the site of a military airfield for the purpose.

Involuntary detention by government is a form of treatment that can be applied over a wide range of coerciveness, from children's homes and open prisons to padded cells and establishments such as the arctic death camps of the Soviet regime (Conquest, 1978). Some governments, of course, are much more heavy-handed with such forms of treatment than others; none does without them altogether.

In the United Kingdom, government turned to compulsory detention on a large scale in the nineteenth century, when transportation to the colonies went out of favour and execution came to be seen as an inappropriate punishment for petty crime. A fashion then developed for penal servitude as a method for treating adults, and for reformatory schools to apply the custodial principle to neglected or criminal children. Indeed, in the late nineteenth century the British Home Office even went so far as to extend the approach to alcoholism, by establishing special government reformatories to which habitual drunkards could be sentenced, involving the compulsory deprivation of alcohol for as much as three years. Needless to say, the scheme was a total failure (Troup, 1925, p. 182).

Much of this nineteenth-century apparatus of reformatories and custodianship is still intact and there are recent additions as well. The keeping of individuals under some form of constraint is a form of treatment which tends sorely to tax capacity (the limit of 'organisation'), especially when large numbers are involved; but it is not likely to disappear as an instrument of government.

Transportation and distribution

A third method of treatment is transportation and distribution, the latter in the sense of direct physical allocation rather than in the tokens-of-authority sense of quota enablements.

Government moves and physically distributes a broad range of items. It may remove the garbage from each home. It may supply individuals with building materials for putting up houses and farmsteads in remote areas. It may physically distribute ballot papers to each registered voter in an election – a device originally introduced in the last century to prevent abuse of the secret ballot in the form of bribing voters to deposit in the ballot-box voting papers that had been marked outside the polling station (Etzioni-Halevy, 1979).

Government frequently uses transportation and distribution as a front-line instrument for tackling natural and other disasters, when it moves items like blankets, food and medical supplies to the victims. Governments have distributed food and grain to their subjects from their storehouses during times of shortage since the days of the ancient Oriental despotisms (Wittfogel, 1959), and modern governments may find themselves undertaking physical distributions in a variety of 'crisis' situations. For example, the Spanish government distributed large quantities of cooking oil after many of its subjects had been poisoned by contaminated cooking oil in 1980.

Civil emergencies of a rather different kind may also cause government to draw on its organisational capacity for transportation and distribution. Governments may choose to move important supplies as a means of strike-breaking, as did the British government when it moved food from the docks during the General Strike of 1926 (and it has used similar treatment in response to a number of subsequent strikes).

Sometimes it is people rather than goods that government chooses to move and distribute. From the time of the loss of its American colonies until 1867, the British government transported convicts to Australia. In many cases, of course, government causes people to move by means of official tokens such as deportation orders. But, if only as a last resort, government will sometimes do the job itself. Even the most liberal of governments will from time to time have to undertake the forcible deportation of individuals who do not find favour with the authorities.

Processing

A fourth major way in which government may apply treatment is to change the state of something rather than to mark, store or move it. This, too, is applied by government in a wide range of circumstances, from more or less unexceptionable everyday services to repression of the most outright kind.

An example of the former type is the role sometimes taken by government in destroying wasp nests, insect infestations, rats, mice or more exotic creatures in those circumstances where using authority, in the form of orders on the relevant owner or occupier to clear his/her property of the pest in question, will not do the job. Activities such as these bring the relevant agriculture departments in Britain into the news from time to time, for example during periods of cattle plague or when scares arise from the introduction of exotic pests such as the Colorado beetle into ports and other areas.

Sometimes it is propagation rather than destruction that government seeks through treatment. A traditional example is those government-run stud farms to which citizens can, on payment of the appropriate fee, send horses of either sex to be mated with government's breeding animals. In 1981 the French government had over 1500 breeding stallions for this purpose (*The Times*, 11 July 1981). This is, of course, a survival from the days when government took a close interest in the breeding of bloodstock in order to ensure a supply of good quality horses to serve as cavalry mounts in time of war.

From government processing of goods or animals to processing the persons of its individual subjects is a step which begins to take us away from common or garden government services. But even here there is a range of applications, from the prison haircut or the vaccination through compulsory sterilisation or frontal lobotomy to the firing squad or the disposal of the dead in government crematoria and cemeteries.

Law enforcement, political repression, the punishment of those defined as criminals or deviants, typically make heavy use of this form of treatment. All governments must be equipped forcibly to arrest their subjects in certain circumstances, if only to enforce the judgements of law courts. Beyond that, of course, governments vary enormously in their use of such instruments. Some governments in the twentieth century have chosen to execute their subjects in massive numbers – a process too depressingly familiar to need extensive illustration. The million or so executions carried out in the People's Republic of China between 1945 and 1953 and the million or so carried out during the 'cultural revolution' of the 1960s (Rosenberg and Young, 1982) are just two of the well known examples.

Variations in the use of this kind of processing are not only a matter of the differing readiness of different governments to reach for weapons to punish their political enemies. The point at which such treatment is triggered also varies widely. In the Soviet Union, to take an extreme case, those who have committed crimes such as 'economic sabotage' in the form of corruption or fraud, may find themselves being executed by the government. Those who have criticised the government in public may find themselves being subjected to a course of 'psychiatric treatment' in a government mental hospital (since public criticism is seen as a clear sign of insanity).

There is, in fact, a grim catalogue of such 'treatments' by government, which includes flogging and mutilation (still used as punishments by some governments) and prison punishments – the modern-day equivalent of the tread-wheel and the crank, formally abandoned in British prisons in 1898. Few governments nowadays admit to practising outright torture, in contrast to the days of the seventeenth century, when using the thumb-screw on suspected conspirators was regarded as a legitimate instrument of government. But what is admitted and what is practised are not the same; and, at the least, diminutives of torture are used by all governments.

Group treatment

The last section discussed the application of government treatment to the persons or property of particular individuals. That discussion was intended to convey some indication of the enormous range of applications to which government's 'organisation' can be put, stretching from the comparatively trivial to fundamental matters of life and death. Of course, government can apply treatments in a more general way as well; and, just as has been shown for other kinds of effectors in previous chapters, there is an intermediate point at which government may direct its efforts towards groups rather than to particular individuals or to the world at large. *Group treatment* is something practised by governments since very early times, notably the burning or destruction of a whole settlement as a form of 'group punishment' for the acts of some of the inhabitants. It is by no means in desuetude today, and there are many possible applications; but an example or two must suffice here.

One example is group transportation. For good or bad reasons, governments sometimes transport social groups rather than aggregations of individuals. Governments often find themselves involved in evacuating refugee groups from a place of danger or deprivation by means of airlifts and the like. The British government's first experience of this kind of activity in modern times came in 1930, when it evacuated the entire population of the remote Scottish island of St Kilda, using a naval vessel (Steel, 1975).

Another example is crowd control, in which government applies treatment to a group as an entity, rather than to any particular individual, employing methods such as police baton charges, tear gas, water cannon, plastic or real bullets fired into the crowd. But there is, of course, a narrow line between 'treating the group' and treating the world at large.

At-large treatment

'Group treatment' is a half-way house between the general and the particular. *At-large treatment* is treatment applied by government to the world at large or to whomever it may concern. Examples of 'at-large treatment' are the man-trap (and its modern extension into devices which automatically trap illegally parked vehicles) and involuntary methods of disinfection (such as footbaths built into the entry to swimming-pools or disinfecting pads placed across farm gateways to prevent the spread of animal disease. Other examples are the putting of fluoride in domestic water supplies or all the grisly techniques that modern governments are able to deploy for large-scale homicide. Such applications of organisation are in a sense 'general' and thus loosely correspond to general applications of other basic government resources, such as propaganda or standard constraints, which have already been discussed.

Government may 'treat' us in the mass by altering the physical environment in which we operate rather than by getting to work on us as individuals (elsewhere I have termed this 'ergonomic control' – Hood,

1976, pp. 118–20). Government may provide for the welfare of its subjects in general by facilities such as parks, gardens, bridges, dykes and dams. It may cover the landscape with towers and gateways, roads and barriers (Lasswell and Fox, 1979). It may exhibit its collections of art treasures, documents, property, land or animals, for anyone who wishes to see them.

Similarly, governments have always employed construction projects, altering the world at large, as part of their basic equipment for coping with enemies or insurgents. Modern governments experiment with methods of 'weather control', by cloud shepherding and the like. A more traditional example of at-large treatment' is the government wall, such as the Great Wall of China, the Roman walls, the 'Flodden wall' built round Edinburgh in the sixteenth century and the Berlin wall of our own times.

Wittfogel (1959) aruges that 'at-large treatment' in the form of big construction projects was one of the most basic instruments used by the great oriental despotisms of antiquity, and other types of governments also rely heavily on this device on occasion. For example, after defeating a rebellion by Jacobite forces in 1715, the British government undertook a massive road-, canal-, fort- and bridge-building programme in Scotland, in the hope that this would enable government to defeat future rebellions more easily. The programme was carried out entirely by government's own troops until 1790, after which government adopted the more common modern practice of relying on outside contractors for construction projects (Haldane, 1962, p. 19). In other words, there was a switch away from 'organisation' to 'treasure' for the job.

The architecture of 'defensible space' (Newman, 1972) as a means of general treatment is basic to government, but new applications are constantly appearing. For example, the upsurge of rebelliousness by university students in the 1960s led several governments to search for ways of moving away from the traditional one-campus physical layout of universities in order to make it more difficult for student revolutionaries to paralyse the organisation by seizing a single key point. Similarly, there are signs of governments becoming more self-conscious again about incorporating crime prevention into the architecture of public places, for example by brightly lit wide open spaces with no hiding places, no paving stones for rioters to tear up, spaced-apart car parking and vandal-proof street furniture.

Much of government's at-large treatment is, of course, fairly humdrum: clearing snow, treating sewage, lighting streets. Often, however, such physical operations may form the keystone of a wider administrative arch. A well known example is the device of the fiscal monopoly, in which government monopolises the production of a key item like tobacco or salt as a revenue-raising device (instead of granting licences to others to do so, as in the tax-farming mode). Sometimes such monopolies are highly specific, resting on a narrow point in the production process. An interesting case is the early attempt to impose taxes on playing cards in Britain, which involved printing the Ace of Spades separately at the government printing office. The penalty for anyone using any Ace of Spades other than those printed by the government was originally death (Olmstead, in Herman (ed.), 1967, p. 139), though the sentence was later reduced to transportation, and later still, in 1861, to penal servitude for life.

The tool-set in context

From the comments that have been made about other classes of government's tools in previous chapters, the reader should now be well primed to notice several things for him- or herself about the use of treatment by government.

The administration of treatment

The range of examples in the first part of the chapter was intended to convey an impression of the variety of ways in which government can put 'organisation' to work. 'Treatment' or direct action is an everyday tool of government. It figures, of course, in most if not all of government's operations in the form of the 'long-stop' of physical law enforcement. Apart from that, its use varies widely from one area of policy to another. Some areas of government operations tend to be heavy on treatment (such as public health, where government may be involved in emptying cesspits, removing refuse and night-soil, sweeping streets and processing sewage, providing public lavatories and baths, and so on); others tend to be light (such as the control of charities or financial institutions, which typically requires no more than an occasional invoking of physical law enforcement). Other areas may involve heavy resort to treatment only intermittently (such as labour relations, when government may periodically become involved in breaking strikes and taking over the jobs of strikers).

However, in some ways government's use of treatment is a little different from the effectors considered in the last three chapters, especially those based on nodality and authority. As we have seen, these are employed by almost every government agency to some degree and may be inextricably tangled up with one another, so that the same agency or government official might continually turn from using one tool to another, just as the surgeon must be able to turn readily from probe to scalpel to forceps.

There are, of course, exceptions, as has already been noted. But treatment, by and large, is not like that. Many government agencies, such as regulatory offices, which rely principally on nodality and authority to perform their tasks, do not use it at all. Many if not most direct government employees never perform any treatments at all (Simon, Smithburg and Thompson, 1950, p. 443). The use of violence and the physical treatment of individuals (in prison, for example) tend to be concentrated in units that are separated from general purpose bureaucratic operations even in quite early systems of government (Fagen, 1966, pp. 131–2, n. 5). The same often applies to uses of treatment in other, less dramatic ways, which are often concentrated in 'common service' agencies or units rather than deployed directly by all government agencies.

Combinations and substitutions

Another theme which is by now familiar is government's ability to link different kinds of effecting tool together. Government can combine treatments, both sequentially and simultaneously, in many different ways for the tasks it wishes to carry out. For example, it may respond to natural disasters such as floods, earthquakes or landslips by individual treatments (distribution, processing), by group treatment (such as evacuation), by at-large treatments (re-modelling the landscape), or by some mixture of all three. It may repress dissent by treating 'dangerous' individuals, by concentrating on groups, or by at-large treatments such as the erection of defensive walls.

Equally, government may substitute one kind of tool for another at two levels. First, it may substitute onc form of treatment for another. For example, when government physically alters capital cities or football stadia to make crowd control easier (such as by digging a moat or building a wall around a football field, or by caging spectators with chain-link fences to stop them from running on to the field in order to attack players or the referee), it is using at-large treatment in an attempt to take some pressure off group and individual treatment.

Second, direct action may be substitutable for the other types of effectors that have been discussed in previous chapters. In Chapter 2 an example was given of government to some extent substituting information-dispensing for direct action in the policing of an unruly crowd. Indeed, there are many cases where the effective use of information may make treatment unnecessary. But the opposite is also the case. Instead of using nodality to influence people's minds, government may use treatment to change their bodies or their environment. For example, instead of exhorting motorists to drive slowly through residential streets, government can have 'sleeping policemen' (ridges) built into the road so that high speed can only be achieved at the cost of a heavy toll on the driver's nerves or expensive wear and tear on his vehicle. Instead of trying to persuade squatters to leave the property they are occupying, government can cut off the water, electricity and gas supplies to vacant properties. Instead of propaganda campaigns to encourage children to take care of their teeth, government can fluoridate the water supply.

Direct action may similarly be substitutable for the use of moneys or tokens of authority. The choice for government between contract and 'do-it-yourself' was discussed in Chapter 3, and even 'treasure-heavy' governments may want to choose the latter in some circumstances. For example, the US Army Corpos of Engineers occasionally undertakes difficult or dangerous civil engineering work itself where no tender for the job is forthcoming at a reasonable price.

The same goes for tokens of authority. For example, instead of forbidding grafitti in public places, government can coat the relevant walls with a surface on which it is impossible to write, or from which writing can easily be erased. Instead of forbidding glue-sniffing, government might treat glue in such a way as to make it unattractive to sniffers. It can require unfit meat to be stained or do the job itself, just as it can operate its own slaughterhouses or set standards for the slaughtering of meat.

Treatment and direct action: protases

What circumstances may cause government to switch its emphasis from one kind of treatment to another, or its overall emphasis on treatment relative to its other effectors? No general answer can be attempted here; but as in previous chapters, two main factors will be picked out as liable to influence goverment's treatment 'mix'. They are the size of populations involved, and the wider social context (of consensus or the opposite) within which government operates.

(1) *Size of population.* By now the reader will be accustomed to the idea that (ignoring any revenue or output effects and looking only at the absolute administrative costs) some tools may be more expensive for government to use than others, in terms of the administrative effort and cost involved.

Just as applies to the government instruments discussed in previous chapters, 'particular' types of treatment will tend to be more expensive for government to use than 'general' types where the population is large. Where the numbers involved are very small, it may well be less expensive for government to operate on the individuals concerned than to change their environment in a general way. But there is likely to come a point at which the balance of advantage is reversed, and government then has to weigh up the extra discrimination among its subjects that may be achieved by using individual treatments against the extra bureaucratic effort that is involved. As we have seen, capacity is heavily taxed when government tries to imprison large numbers of people, and the same goes for other kinds of individual treatment.

Moreover, for reasons that will be explored more closely in Chapter 8, if revenue effects are laid aside, direct action or treatment is in some ways a more expensive instrument for government to use than instruments based on nodality or authority, since it rests on a resource which in its nature has to be re-supplied or replenished as it is used. (The same applies to moneys, as has already been pointed out.) Possibly for this reason, government is often on the look-out for ways of substituting other tools for treatment.

For example, from 1919 until 1971, the British government itself disinfected all imported goat-hair and goods mixed with goat-hair as a means of preventing the disease of anthrax. At its height, this was a major factory operation, handling millions of pounds-weight of goat-hair per year. But in 1971, when looking for ways of cutting costs, the government switched to a different instrument, replacing organisation with authority. It simply banned the import of goods such as goat-hair that were liable to be infected with anthrax unless they were sent for disinfection to private-sector factories approved by government (*Department of Employment Gazette*, 1971, p. 819).

(2) *The wider social context.* The social context is also likely to affect the mix of tools that government adopts, as we have seen in earlier chapters. Thus in conditions of consensus or of general acceptance of its regime, government may be able to use direct action tools sparingly. Information, official tokens or the cheque-book will often suffice as effectors in these circumstances. Government can reserve the typically more expensive tools of direct action for the emergency, the exceptional case, or the activity especially dear to its heart. Many have remarked that government, certainly on the modern scale, would be impossible if no activity could be induced from its subjects except by applying coercion to each individual.

As consensus and acceptance decline, however, government will be decreasingly able to rely on its other effectors alone. Indeed, as we have seen, there comes a point at which government's official tokens and demands for payment are flouted, its messages fall on deaf or hostile ears, and its cheque-book fails to buy physical support. In those circumstances, government has to switch increasingly to direct action tools, being obliged to turn to the most expensive kinds of instruments just at the point when its resources are likely to be under the heaviest pressure.

Moreover, as government comes under pressure, experiencing increasing resistance to its regime, it may find itself having to turn from individual treatments in the direction of at-large ones. As the pressure mounts, discrimination may become decreasingly possible. The innocent must be lumped with the guilty, the bystander with the committed rebel. Instead of individual treatments, government may come to place more emphasis on treatments that address the populace in the mass, dealing with crowds or groups in military-style operations or undertaking general environmental changes to influence social behaviour by 'ergonomic' means.

This, too, may serve to reduce still further the overall level of social acceptance within which government operates. This is partly because in such circumstances government is no longer distinguishing effectively between its enemies and its friends or non-combatants, and partly because activities such as the ones mentioned above may bring the darker side of government's tool-bag into greater exposure. This can be dangerous for government. Governments like to be coy about their use of violence against the person, even though that is an inescapable part of the tool-bag of any government – part of its defining characteristics, in fact. Often it is kept out of sight or obscured by euphemistic phraseology such as I discussed in Chapter 2 (for example, the British government forces deployed to quell riots in prisons are termed, with perhaps a touch of irony, 'Minimum Use of Force Tactical Intervention Squads'). But when direct action becomes government's mainstay or its only usable instrument, this side of its activities becomes harder to conceal.

Direct action, in the form of the use of force against their subjects, is said to be 'the last argument of princes'. But it is a very expensive way for government to argue. And it is expensive in a sense rather different from the bureaucracy-intensive costs of using tools such as customised payments or direct notification. That is precisely because it *is* the last argument of princes. If the final shot in government's locker fails to go home, nothing else remains.

II HOW GOVERNMENT GETS INFORMATION: DETECTION

Part I of the book looked at government's 'effecting' tools, its instruments for acting upon the world. This part looks at the other side of the picture: that is, how government obtains information about the world outside. As was explained in Chapter 1, to do that it needs *detecting* instruments, using the terminology of cybernetics.

Each of government's four basic resources that were discussed in Chapter 1 (nodality, treasure, authority and organisation) can be used for 'detection' as well as for 'effecting'.

Thus nodality may cause government to receive information in the same way as it may give government a reason to be listened to. People may give government information simply because of its social centrality and visibility – 'because it's there'. Information of this kind is in a sense free for government, and the detectors that pick it up are here called *nodal receivers*.

Similarly, government's second resource of treasure can be used to buy information. This kind of detector is here termed *rewards*, but it goes a little beyond treasure in a narrow sense, denoting information which government gets in return for any kind of tangible *quid pro quo*.

Third, government can use its legal authority and demand information. This kind of detector is termed *requisitions*, to mean information that is collected in the form of an official demand (characteristically accompanied by threatened sanctions for non-compliance). Fourth, government can use its organisation to get information, in the form of physical or mechanical contrivances for scrutiny which largely by-pass human motivation. These are here called *ergonomic detectors*.

TABLE II.1 Government detectors

	Nodal receivers	Rewards	Requisitions	Ergonomic detectors
Passive (government at a fixed point or not taking initiative ↑	Unsolicited tenders (unconditional)	Unsolicited propositions	Obligations to display	Turnstiles
	Ear trumpet	Advertised rewards	Obligations to notify	Fixed scanners
		Applications (information as a by-product)	Returns	
	Scrutiny of free media (active search within government offices)	Information exchange (subjects pool information with government for mutual benefit)	Interrogation (active search, but informant required to attend on government)	Mobile scanners
↓ Active (government operating away from home or taking initiative)	Direct inquiry (government waits on informant)	Active propositions (made by government to prospective informant)	Inspections	Hidden scanners

In fact, the parallel between these four types of detector and the four types of effector discussed in Part I of the book is by no means exact, as will be seen. But it is close enough to serve as a starting point, so that the reader can 'place' the discussion of detectors in relation to that of effectors.

However, when it comes to government detection, it makes less sense to distinguish between particular and general applications. Instead, the emphasis here is laid on the distinction between 'active' and 'passive' modes of government information-gathering. The difference between the two lies in the degree of initiative or mobility that government requires to obtain the information in question. Thus when government observes us from a fixed watchtower, it is passive. When it knocks on our door or stops our car in the street to pursue its inquiries, government is active. Clearly, there are many intermediate points between these two extremes. For simplicity, activity and passivity will here be taken as a combination of initiative and mobility, though it would be possible to take the two separately.

Looking at these four basic types of detector in their active and passive manifestations gives us a way of mapping government's tool-kit for detection. If there were space, each of the four might merit a chapter in itself, as was done for effecting tools; as it is, all four must be looked at in a single chapter. In order to help the reader follow the discussion, all of the detection devices that will be considered in Chapter 6 are set out in Table II.1.

It should perhaps be stressed once more at this point that, just as applied to effectors, the interest here is exclusively on the instruments that government uses at its interface with the world outside. When it comes to detection, that means we are interested only in the tools by which government extracts information from its subjects. We do not consider how that information is used or processed (or not, as the case may be) within government's machine. There are many fascinating things to be said about that process, but they will not be said here. We are concerned with ingestion, not digestion.

6 Tools for Detection

Is a true Briton to have no privacy? Are the fruits of his labour and toil to be picked over, farthing by farthing, by the pimply minions of Bureaucracy?

(quoted in Sabine, 1966, p. 31)

Up to now, we have been looking at 'effecting'. But much of 'what government does' consists of obtaining information in one way or another. Thus government needs a set of tools for examination, inspection, monitoring, watching and detecting, tools which must be applicable to a wide range of objects.

It is instructive to consider for a moment just how wide that range is. Government must scrutinise human beings in many circumstances, sometimes by means of direct physical inspection, as in the case of potential recruits to the civil service or to the army, or by means of other body searches conducted *à l'outrance*, more commonly by less literal forms of examination. Government must also be equipped to scrutinise a wide variety of non-human items. It examines animals and plants in order to establish fitness to travel or to certify breeding stock. It examines documents of all kinds. It scans the skies for aircraft, spacecraft, missiles, radio transmissions and weather patterns. It continually surveys areas within its own territory (and, of course, areas within the territories of other governments) by photographing and mapping. It examines a host of inanimate objects for a wide variety of purposes, some mundane, others exotic.

This is the very briefest glimpse of government's detecting activities, but it does serve to give an impression of the range of detecting equipment that is used at the boundary between government and the outside world.

Because the whole range of government's detectors are dealt with in this chapter, it is a little longer than the chapters in Part I, but otherwise follows the same pattern. That is, it begins with a brief inventory of government detecting tools, going through the four main types shown in Table II.1. The second part is a discussion of how government's detectors are coupled with one another in action, and the circumstances that may prompt government to use one kind of detector rather than another.

Nodal receivers

Everyone knows the aphorism about a free lunch. There's no such thing. But some lunches are certainly cheaper than others. It is the same with information. Some information can be obtained virtually free, by doing no more than inserting oneself as a 'node' in an information network. This is the kind of information that is picked up by what are here called 'nodal receivers'. As the name implies, government is here relying mainly on its resource of 'nodality' centrality, visibility, interconnectedness – with its other resources only in the background.

The most passive kind of nodal receiver picks up information that is volunteered spontaneously. We can label this kind of detection *unsolicited tenders*. This is information that government obtains, not by diligent search, but simply by maintaining a passive presence. Government does not have to pump or prime and certainly does not pay for such information in any direct sense, except perhaps in terms of the amount of time involved.

Even as individuals, we receive a lot of information in this way, from the bore, the busybody, the advertiser, and so on; and the more 'nodal' we are, the more we are likely to receive. To government this will typically apply all the more: its nodality means that it will obtain information of some kind even if it does nothing but drink in what is offered in the form of unsolicited tenders.

Information obtained in this way will naturally be of varying types. It may be warnings, threats or criticisms from other governments or bodies such as business lobbies or labour unions. It may be information about specific wrongdoing, offered by busybodies, maleficiaries or rivals of the individual or organisation concerned. It may be 'free samples' of information, sent to government in the hope of tempting it to pay for more. It may even be information prompted by public-spiritedness, as in the case of individuals who tell government about the flying saucers that they have seen or of inventors (such as Henry Bell, the builder of the first steamship) who spontaneously send details of their work to government in the belief that it may be of interest. (The British government, of course, treated Bell's information with 'cold neglect' (Mitchell, 1971, p. 131), as plainly irrelevant to naval warfare.)

Perhaps we might say that in a certain sense information of this type is offered for a reward. But the informer's reward in these cases lies in Heaven, in the propagation of a cause, in the hope of seeing another's discomfiture, or in other forms too complicated to probe here. The point is that government does not have to pay directly for information of this type, and this may be important, especially when public feelings are running high.

Similarly, to describe information of this type as 'free' to government is to ignore what economists in their language call opportunity costs: that is, what might otherwise have been done with the time involved. The cost to government of this kind of information lies, of course, in the screening process that it must undertake to separate the gold from the dross.

'Ear trumpet'

Certainly, when information has to be actively sought, it ceases to be 'free' in an even more obvious sense. But government can still obtain information on the basis of its nodality alone (that is, without needing to reward, demand or physically constrain), even when it is active. The first stage of this comes when government starts to prompt its subjects to come to it with information.

By doing this, government can remain passive in the sense of being an immobile observer (no bureaucrat need leave his or her office) while making itself highly receptive to incoming information and encouraging the public to act as informers. Machine tools such as answering machines and telephone hotlines are common devices used by government to make itself highly accessible to incoming information. These provide channels by which individuals can give information anonymously without the problems and perhaps dangers from hostile sources that a face-to-face encounter with government bureaucracy may involve. Government is not, of course, alone in using such devices: they are ubiquitous, from the radio phone-in programme to the hotlines for troubled individuals that are maintained by voluntary organisations. The reply-paid postcard is another form of the same general device.

This tactic is here termed *ear trumpet* – an old-fashioned kind of hearing aid consisting of a large trumpet held against the ear and directed at whoever was speaking. 'Ear trumpet' is the 'prompted query response' device of Chapter 2 turned inside out, and it is a device that is widely used by government bureaucracies in practice. For example, it is a notable theme of Cranston's (1979) study of the enforcement of consumer legislation in Britain. The British public has been encouraged to act as government spies against businessmen by complaining to local consumer advice centres or price regulation offices (e.g. during the Second World War and in subsequent price control schemes); more recently, they have been encouraged by government to 'blow the whistle' on neighbours whom they suspect to be welfare scroungers, fraudulently claiming benefit payments. Similarly, the US General Accounting Office has used a 'freefone' system for members of the public to volunteer information about waste and misappropriation within the agencies monitored by the GAO.

Scrutiny of free media and direct inquiries

Of course, government can insert itself as a 'node' into an information system by means considerably more direct than the 'ear trumpet' device. *Scrutiny of free media* is one such means. This device does not depart from the passive mode in the sense that it need not involve working outside government's offices. Government officials commonly devote considerable care to scrutinising media sources, both of the general kind and of specialist types such as trade journals or special interest magazines. Thus a local newspaper story of an individual losing a large sum of cash through housebreaking will be read with interest by the local tax inspector to see if it tallies with that individual's tax records (*Taxation*, 1964).

The most active kind of nodal receiver is *direct inquiry*. Here government officials go out 'into the streets', as it were, and request information from people directly, though still without employing any overt reward or threat. For example, during the Second World War the British government became worried that psychological warfare and enemy bombing of the cities would erode public morale, causing confidence in the government to collapse and fostering a mutinous or revolutionary spirit. As a result, an agency known as 'Cooper's Snoopers' (Ogilvy-Webb, 1965, pp. 61–2) was set up to conduct questionnaire surveys among the general public to discover their attitudes. This was, in fact, the origin of the present-day government polling service in Britain. Nowadays government conducts a host of surveys among the population at large (ranging from general attitude surveys to more specific surveys of family expenditure and the like) which differ from the traditional government census in that the questions are not compulsory.

Rewards

Nodal receivers, through which government picks up information for which it does not have to pay directly, are an important part of government's detection repertoire. This will apply especially in certain circumstances, for example when feelings of patriotism have been whipped up or after an unusually shocking crime or accident. Perhaps, in some ideal administrative world, it might be desirable to conduct all of government's detection in this way. In reality, of course, government has to use resources other than nodality alone in order to obtain information. The term 'rewards' denotes information which government 'buys', offering some positive incentive. Often this involves the use of government's 'treasure' in a strict sense, but rewards for information may be in forms other than straightforward cash payment.

Unsolicited propositions

As in the case of nodal receivers, government may draw in information for reward in more than one way. The most passive mode is for government to wait to be approached by individuals or organisations offering information for a *quid pro quo*, as happens in those cases where officials of potentially hostile governments offer to defect or to sell secrets in exchange for political asylum or other rewards. This may be termed the *unsolicited proposition*. It differs from the unsolicited tender in that information is spontaneously offered to government, but only on condition that some 'price' is paid.

Advertised rewards and application

Somewhat less passive, and roughly corresponding to the 'ear trumpet' type of nodal receiver, is the case where government obtains information for reward by means roughly analogous to those used by a mail-order firm – that is, by offering its wares and waiting for a response.

There are in fact two forms of this. Government can use the straightforward device of *advertised rewards* for information. The term is self-explanatory, and the obvious case is the wall poster advertising reward for information leading to the capture of criminals or outlaws. Paid tax informers and other types of paid informers play a quantitatively small but nevertheless important part in many types of information-gathering, and in some cases the 'payment' may be in a form more exotic than cash alone.

The other device for drawing in information by publishing rewards is rather less direct. Here information is obtained as a by-product, in that the bait being dangled or being sought is not specifically presented as a reward for information. This type of information-gathering device could be termed *applications*.

Information derived from applications is, of course, a commonplace in government, and it comes about in many diverse forms. If you wish to enter a high-security prison, for example, government may photograph you. If you wish to apply for a patent from government, you must produce extensive plans and drawings. In the United Kingdom, if you are a single mother applying for welfare benefits, government may choose to ask you a battery of questions on the most intimate details of your past sex life. In the 1970s the British government learned a great deal about the incidence of child handicap (a subject on which it was highly ignorant) by offering money to the families of handicapped children and analysing the characteristics of those who applied (Bradshaw, 1980).

Indeed, whenever government disburses its treasure as 'contracts' or 'transfers', it typically requires the prospective recipient to supply information in order to establish qualification or eligibility. Government seldom gives out money 'with no questions asked', thus denying itself the possibility of obtaining information as a by-product. Applications can, of course, be of varying spontaneity. The more government begins to prompt, with widespread advertising of the benefits that can be applied for and the like, the less passive the process becomes.

Information exchange and active propositions

An interesting sub-type of the device of obtaining information for reward, falling somewhere on the boundary of passive and active (and indeed of information-dispensers and detectors), is the *information exchange*. In this case, the sole reward for supplying information lies in access to the pool of data which is created by a number of individuals or organisations acting in this way for mutual benefit. The classic case of this, of course, is the marriage bureau or dating agency. In the government sphere, the labour exchange or job placement agency is a somewhat similar device, to the extent (rather limited in practice) that it is a voluntary pool of information created by potential sellers and buyers of labour. The pure information exchange is a very rare tool in government, but approximations to it are not unknown.

Rewards as detecting tools become more active when it is government that approaches potential informants proffering gifts rather than vice versa. The analogy shifts from the mail-order house to the doorstep salesman. The *active proposition* by government corresponds to the 'direct inquiry' mode in nodal receivers, except that in the latter case government's subjects are neither required to answer the questions nor rewarded for doing so. Direct inquiries rely on the informant's good nature or sense of self-importance. When it uses active propositions, government is appealing to the informant's self-interest in a more straightforward way.

The term 'propositioning' is here intended to be neutral. It does not necessarily imply any kind of impropriety. Propositioning can take perfectly respectable and conventional forms, as normally applies when government seeks out particular individuals or organisations to offer rewards for consultancy or expert information. Of course, there *are* 'exotic' forms as well. Government may use sexual lures to obtain information, especially from foreign embassy staff (so-called 'swallows', for example KGB 'chambermaids', Cuban counter-intelligence prostitutes, and so on). All sorts of other rewards may be profferred in the cloak-and-dagger world of spies and defectors. Like the information exchange, active propositioning is not all that common in the whole range of government detectors, although it may well be very important in some cases.

Requisitions

'Requisitions' are those kinds of detector that are based principally on government's resource of legal authority. Instead of obtaining information by nodality or by exchange, government requires it, under threat of sanction for non-compliance.

Here again, there is a spectrum from 'passive' to 'active'. One common passive method can be termed the *obligation to display*. Here government requires subjects of certain classes or types to display identification symbols so that they can be spotted or counted by the use of fairly passive methods (there is, of course, a fine line between requiring others to display and government doing the marking itself, which was discussed in Chapter 5). Government may oblige the population at large to carry identity symbols in the form of cards, papers, bracelets and the like. For example, in 1980 the Hong Kong government required its subjects to wear identity discs, as part of a crackdown on illegal immigration from the People's Republic of China.

Personal identification is a highly charged issue. The device also has more humdrum applications, as when airlines require us to put identity tags on our luggage. Motor vehicles are required not only to be registered with the government (a process that will be discussed shortly), but also to have their registration numbers prominently displayed so that the number can be seen from a distance. In some countries discs or stickers denoting payment of tax or safety inspections also have to be displayed on the windscreen or number-plate. Other applications of the principle are the load-lines that must be displayed by merchant ships, or the registration numbers that must be displayed by fishing boats and aircraft.

Obligation to display is closely linked to the use of tokens of authority to compel government's subjects to display certain information, such as food ingredients or the kinds of chemicals being carried by road tankers, to the general public (as distinct from the forces of government alone). The two often overlap, and indeed such an overlap may sometimes strengthen government detection. Simon, Smithburg and Thompson (1950, p. 479) describe how persons allocated extra petrol rations on account of their occupation in the USA during the Second World War were obliged to paste a sticker on the windscreen of their car, in the hope that anyone who was not really entitled to extra rations would be betrayed to the authorities by his or her neighbours.

Obligation to notify

A more common method by which government can obtain information by requiring it under threat of sanction, while still retaining a relatively passive detection stance, is the *obligation to notify*. Government insists on certain items being brought to its notice, as opposed to having symbols displayed in case it chooses to notice them. For example, it may require men in a certain age group to register for military draft purposes.

There are many varieties of this device. Sometimes we are required to give government prior notification of a course of action that we plan to take, as applies to alterations to land or buildings. Sometimes we are required to notify government *post hoc*, telling the authorities about some event after it has taken place. The 'notifiable incident' is an information-gathering tool in very common use by government, applying to items such as transport and industrial accidents, mishaps at licensed nuclear installations – even, in the case of cattle plague, to mere suspicions, which British farmers are obliged by law to report to the police. Notification requirements of this kind typically act as triggers for a different mode of information-gathering to be set in train.

Public registration is an example of the 'obligation to notify tool' which goes back to very ancient times. The most familiar example (because everyone is involved in it at some time in their lives) is the registration of births, deaths and marriages, first made compulsory in Britain in 1837. In many other countries government's subjects are also required to register their current address with the police.

Registration schemes in fact exist throughout government's sphere of interest, sometimes extending into less familiar areas. Central government in Britain registers everything from mink and coypu breeders to merchant seamen and independent schools: at the time of writing, farriers have just been added to the list, and the government is threatening to add marriage bureaux to the collection. An example from the USA is the requirement for foreign lobbyists to register with the Justice Department, as a means of identifying public relations firms and consultants purveying propaganda and 'disinformation' on behalf of foreign governments without revealing the identity of their paymasters. Most schemes of business regulation include as part of their standard equipment a requirement that firms operating in the industry concerned must register with government; and in the extreme case, government may require certain types of information to be submitted to itself and to no one else. For example, during the Second World War the British government prohibited employers from notifying job vacancies to any source or medium other than government labour exchanges (Barnes and Reid, 1980, p. 9).

Registration in this sense does not necessarily carry any 'enablement', in the sense that that term was used in Chapter 4. In practice, of course – as a 'social exchange' theorist would be quick to notice – some compulsory registration systems are deliberately mixed in with other types of government benefit, so that in reality there *is* some element of indirect reward for registration. For example, without registration of birth it is difficult to claim government cash benefits or tax offsets in respect of children, and without registration of death it is similarly difficult to claim death benefits or to dispose legally of a dead person's possessions. But registration is not invariably linked to direct rewards for the informant in this way, especially when the informant is an organisation rather than an individual, and government can thus tap into standard operating procedures in a way that may make 'cover ups' expensive (see Hood, 1976, p. 126). British examples include a requirement on television rental companies to inform government of every television rental contract taken out, as a check on the payment of television fees, and a requirement on registered building societies to inform government of every house mortgage that is redeemed, to help government check claims for tax offsets for mortgage interest payments.

Returns

A further tool by which government may require information from the world outside is the *return*, as in the case of returns for income tax or sales tax, a device that is sometimes extended to less familiar items, such as cinema admissions. Returns are very closely linked to obligation-to-notify and compulsory registration systems as information-gathering devices, so that it is difficult to draw a precise boundary.

Part of the distinction between returns and other forms of requisitioned information lies in the frequency or regularity of the process. Returns are obligations to notify government of the state of some system at regular fixed intervals, as in the many cases of monthly, quarterly or annual reports of information that government requires. They can be distinguished from those obligations to notify that are only triggered if and when certain events occur, as in the case of industrial or motor accidents. Many types of government register operate on the irregular, event-triggered, obligation-to-notify principle rather than on returns.

Returns do not only differ from inertia-based, obligation-to-notify systems in the matter of regularity. They are also typically different in that government takes a more active part in the scrutiny process, by sending out standard forms to be sent back by the informant. This is the other sense of 'return'. The classic or text-book case in Britain is the income-tax return that a taxpayer (or non-taxpayer, as the case may be) may receive from government. In such a case the revenue authorities are clearly taking a more active part in the information-gathering process than, say, the registrars of births, deaths and marriages, who require outsiders to make the first approach. But the degree of activity involved is limited: the return mode still lays on the informant the onus of obtaining and producing the information that government desires.

Interrogation and inspection

Information-gathering takes on a greater degree of active search when government not only signals to the informant that information is required (rather than leaving it up to the informant to approach government in certain specified circumstances), but also itself takes on the task of ferreting out the information. All that we, government's subjects, are required to do is to make ourselves (or it may be our property, papers, etc.) available to government for examination.

Two broad types of such information-gathering can be distinguished, differing in terms of the location in which government and its subjects meet. One mode, here termed *interrogation*, requires us (or our property) to attend on government for examination. 'Interrogation' can be used in many different contexts and with varying levels of intensity. It ranges from cases such as the dental estimates examination (to which all state health service patients in Britain are contractually obliged to present themselves if required) to Spanish inquisition-type processes of the kind portrayed in such books as *Nineteen Eighty-Four, Darkness at Noon* and *The Brothers Karamazov*. Government may demand to see our papers or our persons for tax purposes. Its Official Receivers may summon us before them if a bankruptcy petition has been filed against us.

A final type of compulsory government search involves an interrogation process that is still more active in a locational sense – a process that is here termed *inspection*. 'Inspection' involves government playing away from home. It waits on the informant, rather than vice versa. Government may go out compulsorily to inspect factories, retail stores and excise traders. It may seek to locate and compulsorily interview individuals such as bankrupts or schoolchildren (for whom the British government introduced compulsory medical inspections in 1907 – Martin, 1980, p. 97), or even a large part of the adult population, as in the case of the traditional government census. If it takes prisoners of war, it may legally demand certain personal details from them (under the 1949 Geneva Convention). Similarly, it may apply this type of scrutiny to goods or animals rather than to individuals. For example, in the 1840s the British government began the compulsory scientific testing of imported tobacco for adulteration, so as to prevent importers from adulterating imported tobacco for re-export and thus fraudulently claiming replayment of customs duties from government while retaining a portion of the original tobacco for sale in the domestic market (Crombie, 1962, p. 159).

Inspection is a type of information-gathering that corresponds in some ways to the 'direct inquiry' and 'propositioning' modes of inquiry, except that in this case the informant is legally required to answer government's questions, rather than simply invited to tender information on a voluntary basis or offered a reward for doing so. Responses such as 'census refusal' may, and in some cases do, result in fines or imprisonment.

Inspections, like interrogations, can vary widely in frequency, mode of selection and intensity. They range from the routine and predictable mode of government visitation to the raid or sortie, involving intensive search parties coming from out of the blue (as in the case of sudden tax raids, random checks on vehicles or drivers, snap inspections of bank reserve assets, sorties by fishery cruisers, spot searches and locker checks in prisons).

Ergonomic detectors

'Requisitions' draw on the specifically government-like resource of authority. We do find some parallels outside government, but they are usually restricted to intra-organisational processes or to contracting parties, as in the case of insurance companies which require their policy-holders, as a contractual condition, to notify the company of events such as ill-health, criminal convictions and changes of property. The problem with requisitions, of course, is just the same as applies to tokens of authority as effectors. It is one thing to command or to require, another to see that those commands or requests are actually obeyed. Requisitioning information is not costless or foolproof. If it were, government would need no other tools for gathering information.

The fourth main class of information-gathering tool, *ergonomic detectors*, draws mainly on government's resource of organisation – notably equipment and trained staff. Instead of relying mainly on nodality, rewards or authority, government can put the emphasis on physical or mechanical – that is, 'ergonomic' – devices for obtaining information involuntarily or without the co-operation of the informant. Indeed, it has no alternative but to use such means when the object of scrutiny is non-human (or when there is no human medium through which the information may be obtained). Examples include land surveys, forensic science and the observation of weather patterns.

Turnstiles and fixed scanners

To look for passive modes of collecting information involuntarily is to move on to rather slippier ground than for the three other main types of detector. But in one sense one can conceive of passive applications, to the extent that government is strategically placed to watch from a fixed point, even if the strategic placing involved requires the sort of labour and effort needed to put up spy satellites or watchtowers.

The most passive device for involuntary data-gathering is here termed a *turnstile*. This is a detector that is placed in such a way that it is difficult to avoid going past or through it. Modern surveillance systems for the frail elderly in sheltered housing depend on a strip placed under the floor at a key point in such a way that a switch is automatically triggered when the individual under surveillance is active, thus cancelling an alarm signal that would otherwise be sounded after a given period. Many similar examples could be given. Of course, not all 'turnstiles' depend on complicated technology. A traditional example is the gangway system for customs and immigration checks at airports, which simply relies on the routeing of travellers through a bottleneck or turnstile at which customs officials sit.

Whereas a 'turnstile' is a detector so placed that the informant more or less involuntarily goes through, past or over it, a *fixed scanner* is simply a device for convenient observation over some field of potential activity. In that sense it involves a fractionally more active search process than in the case of the 'turnstile'. Effective surveillance from a watchtower (the traditional form of 'fixed scanner') requires an active look-out, whereas a detector at a turnstile has virtually no option but to record the passing of traffic. Just as in the case of turnstiles, the fixed scanner comes in many forms. Some are very simple, such as the large convex mirrors employed by retail stores to help their security staff to catch shoplifters. Others are machine tool developments, covering a wide range of sophistication. Like turnstiles, fixed scanners are an involuntary information-gathering device, in that even if we know that they are watching us, we can only avoid scrutiny by considerable ingenuity or by putting ourselves to some degree of inconvenience.

Mobile scanners and hidden scanners

As has already been indicated, even tools of the type described above can only be termed 'passive' in a certain sense. But they are somewhat more passive than the *mobile scanner*. This is a detector which requires the forces of government to move about in order to conduct involuntary detection. Examples include helicopter surveillance of riots or motor traffic, the roving warships, photographic spotter aircraft and fishery cruisers which governments use for detecting breaches of fishing limits and regulations, or the detector vans used by the British Post Office to identify and locate television sets for which no licence fee has been paid to the government. We can in principle observe such detectors in action if we bother to look, know where to look, or recognise what we are seeing. But, like the fixed scanner and the turnstile, the mobile scanner requires no active co-operation from us. Indeed, such detecting devices are operated on the basic assumption of non-co-operation from the informant.

The final type of detecting tool considered here is the *hidden scanner*. The term refers to detectors that are unobtrusive or deliberately concealed from the informant, like the secret investigations mounted by insurance companies searching for evidence of fraudulent claims (*The Times*, 6 January 1972). Government may choose to steal or copy key documents without the owner's knowledge. It may obtain information by spies and by *agents provocateurs*, as in the case of test purchases of regulated goods, test bets with bookmakers, or inquiries by social security 'snoopers' posing as relatives of those whom they are investigating. In the 1960s 300 officials of the US Federal Bureau of Investigation infiltrated and spied on the 2,500 or so members of the Trotskyite Socialist Workers Party (Lowi and Stone, 1978, p. 27).

Other forms of hidden scanners are secret recorders, telephone taps and similar devices, which involve some sort of 'plant' on the part of government operating outside its own official domain, and are in that sense rather different from the fixed scanner or turnstile. When government uses hidden scanners, it is active in that it attends on the informant, just as in the case of inspections, propositions and direct requests. The difference is that in this case the obligation to supply information is an involuntary one.

Involuntary detection often involves machine tools of a kind that have been developed dramatically in recent times, but as a technique it goes back into the very distant past. Government have always secretly opened mail and listened at keyholes. Indeed, the traditional government monopoly of the carriage of mails was said, on the establishment of a regular post office in Britain in 1657, to be 'the best means to discover and prevent any dangerous and wicked designs against the Commonwealth' (Cmnd 283, 1957, p. 8). Similarly, at one time, government placed heavy reliance on ergonomic detectors such as watchtowers and officials stationed at the gateways of walled towns or at key ports and harbours.

The tool-set in context

It might be tempting here to go into all the sophisticated types of gadgetry that government can deploy for involuntary detection, because there is some fascination in spotting new applications, even though the principle goes back to the 'Ear of Dionysus' in classical antiquity. However, the brief discussion in the last section must suffice, and completes the inventory of government's information-gathering tool-bag.

Having laid out a crude inventory of government's detecting tools, the final part of this chapter will briefly consider, as did each chapter in Part One, how the use of that tool-kit varies from one government agency to another; how the various elements can be coupled to one another and to government's effectors; and the factors which may determine the kind of detection tools that government will pick up.

Comparisons

No two governments employ detectors in exactly the same way. A minimum of international travel leads us to notice that some governments require us to register such things as addresses or apprenticeships while others do not. Similarly, it takes only a modest acquaintance with the machinery of government to realise that government agencies and departments differ widely in terms of the relative use that they make of the various information-gathering instruments discussed here. Some units or agencies use only a single tool. These are usually small or specialised agencies like registry offices, survey or polling agencies. As soon as we come to large and purpose-based government agencies in fields such as health, defence or transport, we will typically find them dipping into most of the tools in government's detection bag. But even here the typical or modal kind of detector will vary from one agency to another.

Two obvious examples of this are income tax and government welfare benefits. The typical detector employed for income tax is the obligation to notify, whereas welfare benefits typically rely on applications – both, significantly, largely passive devices. (Both systems employ a host of other types of detector in supporting roles, of course.) On the other hand, there may be no clear-cut 'modal' form at all in some areas of government detection. Air traffic control is an example: it is built up from a combination of detectors, such as obligation to display, obligation to notify (for example by registration), nodal receivers of various kinds, applications (for permissions to land and the like) and involuntary, fixed-scanner detection.

Combinations and substitutions

Eighteen detectors, as shown in Table II.1, is in one sense a very simple tool-kit. But, as we saw in Part I, a small number of basic components can produce a huge variety of 'hybrid' types if the components are free to combine. In fact, assuming no mutual exclusivities, there are about 6,000 billion possible combinations of the detectors described here, even before we start to think about combinations of detectors and effectors. It is hard to get our minds round that kind of potential complexity.

Like effectors, detectors can be combined both in space and time.

A simple example of spatial combination is the requirement for airline and truck operators to instal mechanical spies to record the movement of their aircraft or vehicles ('black box' flight recorders or tachographs): in this instance there is a linking of ergonomic detectors with requisitions. Equally, it is common for parallel detectors to be used to reinforce one another. For example, when we die, the examination of our financial affairs by the revenue authorities will be cross-checked against the tax that we paid during life. To take another case, government scrutiny of building works (compulsory inspection for soundness of construction, a procedure which in Scotland goes back to the seventeenth century, when wooden and thatched buildings constituted a major fire risk in towns) and rating assessment for property tax may be used to reinforce one another. Each system may be alerted to cases picked up by the other. Indeed, there is much talk nowadays, in the discussion of a 'data bank society', about the possibilities of government putting together information gathered from a number of different detectors for cross-checking and 'picture completion'.

Apart from detectors that reinforce one another in space, government often uses one type of detector to set others in motion, like electrical wiring in series. Relatively passive detectors, such as turnstiles, unsolicited tenders of information, obligatory event-triggered notifications or returns, may trigger off active detectors. For example, returns that are late or missing, or which signal abnormal conditions (such as low liquidity ratios reported by financial institutions) may result in direct inquiry, inspection or interrogation. Even in relatively commonplace and everyday government operations, such as the payment of agricultural livestock subsidies, it is instructive to watch the sequences and combinations of detectors at work. In that case, the physical examination of livestock at abattoirs for weight and quality, and documentary applications for payment by farmers are handled by quite separate agencies in Britain, while the scrutiny of livestock imports and exports brings in yet another agency using a different type of detector.

Not only are government's detectors often linked together in practice; they are also commonly linked with government's effectors. There is an obvious link with information-dispensers, as discussed in Chapter 2: detecting often requires putting information out, whether it is in 'privished' form or the moulding of a whole society by propaganda, so that people will readily volunteer information to government. Similarly, the award of grants and welfare benefits, as we have seen, is closely linked to detection. For example, the population register is linked with official tokens such as tax allowances and passports, which may be denied to those who fail to produce the necessary official certificates.

By and large, detectors and effectors are complementary rather than substitutable, though there may well be circumstances in which more emphasis on detecting may reduce the need for effecting, or in which no more than detection may be needed. By appearing to listen to its subjects, government may distract them from the great affairs of state. And merely requiring people to come before government and answer its questions may on occasion be sufficient for the purpose (this is, for example, the only formal power possessed by the British Royal Fine Art Commissions, which are public-interest 'environment watchdogs' dating from the 1920s).

These are, perhaps, unusual cases. But detection tools may certainly be substitutable for one another, and examples crop up all the time. At the time of writing, the British government is preparing to take its own officials out of the traditional business of examining all personal bankrupts (inspection and interrogation), in favour of a system whereby the task would be done by private-sector bankruptcy receivers nominated and paid for by those petitioning the courts for a bankruptcy order, with simply an obligation-to-notify requirement to tell government of any evidence of fraud (*Bankruptcy: A Consultative Document*, 1980).

Detectors: protases

Finally, what elements might affect the mix of information-gathering tools used by government? Three elements will be considered here, two of which the reader is well acquainted with. They are the size of the population involved, the nature of the task, and the extent to which government rules in a climate of general resistance or consensus.

(1) *Size of population.* In general it may be supposed that the larger the population involved, the more any detection process will have to be passive, unless it is highly selective (as in the case of the lottery system of initiating investigations into possible tax fraud used in Italy with some apparent success in the recent past) or very infrequent, as in the case of government censuses.

The reason for this is that active modes of information-gathering are likely to be relatively expensive for government. This applies even when the information being gained is 'free', in the sense of being produced on request. If all government examinations had to be active, government would be even more expensive and bureaucracy-intensive than it already is – and by a large amount. For example, the 1982 census of the People's Republic of China required a force of census officials roughly double the size of the entire US Federal Civil Service (five million). Not surprisingly, such censuses are infrequent.

By comparison, passive modes of scrutiny will tend to be comparatively cheap. It is not an accident that most government scrutiny relies on information flowing in without too much active penetration of the outside world. Nor is it in the least surprising that the universal stereotype of government detection should be the examination of written applications or required notifications by officials working inside government offices. By operating like this, government throws a large part of the costs of access and of obtaining information on to outsiders, and enables the vast bulk of its detection activities to be done in practice by relatively ill-educated and low-paid staff – considerations which are vital when scrutiny of a large population of items is involved.

(2) *Nature of the task.* The second broad element that is likely to affect government's use of its scrutiny tools is the nature of the task in which it is engaged. There are at least two separate elements of this. First, the inherent visibility of whatever government is looking for, or at, may vary widely, depending on the task involved and the 'standard' for which the detector is operating. At one end of the scale evasion or non-achievement of some standard may necessitate only shallow or minor scrutiny, for example in measuring the land area of a farm or the number of rooms in a house. At the other end of the scale painstaking and long drawn-out inquiry may be needed to test the standard, for example in the checking of computer fraud or of genetic manipulation. Somewhere in the middle of the two extremes of standard visibility would fall cases such as the judgement of individual fitness to work as a key to the payment of sickness benefits (with those familiar problems of evaluating mysterious and unverifiable 'back pains' or mental depression) or bias in selecting pieces of music for playing on radio programmes. The more difficult it is to detect departures from the standard, the more government is likely to have to use active detection tools, or at least to exercise great ingenuity in setting up an effective regime of passive scrutiny.

Another element relating to the nature of the task is the reason for scrutiny, whether it is government's desire to gain something at the expense of the populace, or vice versa. Andrew Dunsire (1978) has classified government operations in these terms, and he names the first type, i.e. where government is demanding something from its subjects, 'collection'. Taxation is, of course, the pure type; and the same applies to those circumstances where government seeks to obtain information by requisition and without offering any direct *quid pro quo*, as in the cases of the census, fingerprinting, identity discs, and the like.

Where the interests of government begin to diverge from those of its individual subjects, nodal receivers may be insufficient to meet government's information needs. Such detectors may work well in heat-of-the-moment situations, in times of ideological fervour, or when the relevant population is significantly divided – for example into *soi-disant* law-abiding traders and 'cowboys' – such that one section will freely inform about the other. Where these conditions are absent, nodal receivers are likely to be unreliable. One could not imagine government's obtaining valid information about its subjects' economic circumstances on a purely voluntary basis, and the same applies to personal identifying characteristics such as race.

The more that the interests of government and its individual subjects diverge, the more government is likely to need to back up passive detection instruments with active ones (such as social security 'snoopers' and tax inspectors) if only *pour encourager les autres*. For example, as fish prices have risen and supplies have become scarcer, the less effective has become the British government's surveillance of the fishing grounds in the indented rocky coastline of the Scottish western highlands. A system of regulation based on a handful of slow fishery cruisers and shore-based inspectors, which may have been reasonably adequate in times when volunteered information was more freely available, is now having to be changed into an increasingly active detection system. Even hidden scanners may come to be deflected by technological counter-measures on the part of the intended informant if the stakes get high enough. If police set up hidden radar speed traps, motorists instal radar detectors in their cars. If government records conversations by hidden bugging devices, people may start carrying pocket radio scramblers.

(3) *The wider social context*. Not only is government's selection of information-gathering tools likely to be constrained by relatively unchangeable technological factors and by more or less constant strategic positions, as in the case of the perpetual battle waged by governments against tax fiddles and social security benefit frauds. The nature of the

or writing only in clichés. Even a drastically limited linguistic repertoire can still produce high combinatorial variety.

The same applies to other hackneyed routines of social behaviour: for example, standard lines of argument, student sit-ins, protest marches and strikes. It is itself a cliché that society nowadays is clichégenic (Zijderveld, 1979), and government bureaucracy is perhaps the ultimate in clichégénic phenomena, with its packages of standard routines, phrases and categories. Like a child's kaleidoscope, each shake produces a different pattern, but the pieces that form the picture stay the same.

The advantage of a language of clichés, of course, is that it is much easier to pick up than a language that is used across its whole range. Master a few key phrases, and what was formerly gibberish quickly becomes readily intelligible. We can 'place' any government activity that we may come across as some combination of the components of a relatively limited tool-kit.

Thinking laterally: identifying alternative tools

Looking at government as a basic tool-set can serve as a variety-generator as well as a variety-reducer; that is, the set can be used as a keyboard capable of producing a very large number of possible combinations and mixes of tools. The 'combinability' of government instruments was a theme running through earlier chapters, with the complexity-generating properties of any 'set' capable of being subjected to combinatorial maths. Even the eight basic types of tools outlined in Chapter 1 can produce over 40,000 combinations, provided there are no mutual incompatibilities in sequence or in space. Divide each of these eight basic types into only two sub-types (say particular and general, or active and passive) and, on the same assumptions, the number of possible mixes runs to over 20,000,000,000,000. To point out the combinatorial implications of further sub-division of the set would only labour the point; already the number of possible states has run away with us.

Such numbers, of course, make no real sense. They would do so only if we had some metric for the number of different situations government faces, so that we could see if the variety in its instruments matched the variety of its environment (as the cybernetic 'Law of Requisite Variety' requires of a viable control system – Beer, 1972, pp. 53–4). The point is merely to demonstrate the variety-generating potential of such a tool-kit.

One of the implications is that no one can systematically work through so many combinations. This is a point that will be taken up in Chapter 8. But browsing round the tool-kit can help to stimulate the process of 'lateral thinking' a little. It can help us to think of alternative ways of tackling a job. It is easy to fall prey to the common assumption that how things are today is how they have always been and that there is no other possible way of going about this or that task.

Apart from combinations, the possibility of substituting some types of government tools for others was another theme of earlier chapters, and several examples of this were given. Look across time and space a little, and the notion that there is a 'natural' government tool for any job is apt to disappear. The government of Elizabeth I of England tried, not very successfully, to support the fishing industry by 'standard constraints', obliging the population at large to eat fish on certain days. The government of Elizabeth II aims (also not very successfully) to do the same thing by a mixture of money-moving to fishermen and a variety of official tokens designed to regulate fishing. In between the two Elizabeths, government has briefly and unsuccessfully gone into the fishing business for itself and tried a number of money-moving devices. Which is the 'natural' instrument?

To consider any public policy question intelligently, we must have at least some idea of what the range of feasible alternative instruments might be. To have a sense of alternatives among which we can choose is, after all, the basis of any kind of rational choice. Oddly, in practice this choice often seems to go by default in government. As Renate Mayntz (1981) observes, 'The choice of [government] instruments . . . is rarely made very consciously and in full realization of the existing alternatives . . . instrument choice is not recognized as a separate step and no criteria are provided for guiding it.'

Types of substitution

In fact, whether they recognise it or not, governments quite frequently engage in a search for substitute instruments for a given task. There are at least three reasons for this, which were mentioned in Chapter 1.

First, so many 'problems' prove stubborn to attack by one set of instruments that governments find themselves looking for a different approach. This happens all the time, and we will come back to this point in the final section of this chapter.

Second, even where there is no perception of an 'effectiveness' problem, government may want to change its mix of tools. For example, a climate of financial stringency and budgetary famine may cause government to look for tools that will do a given job more cheaply than the ones being used at present. The costs to government of using different tools, and the possibility of substituting cheaper for more expensive ones, was a recurring theme in previous chapters, and this question will be looked at more squarely in the next chapter.

A third reason is the fairly common phenomenon of governments searching under the counter, as it were, for instruments to perform some task which for one reason or another government must not be seen to be tackling directly. In such circumstances government finds itself engaged in a process of 'deliberate serendipity'. It looks for tools to use 'out of context', for some unacknowledgeable purpose completely other than that for which they were designed. Government is here using its tool-bag as a 'rummage bag' – a phenomenon that was touched upon in Chapter One.

Sometimes such 'rummaging' is prompted by domestic political circumstances. For years the basis of local government censorship of cinema films in Britain rested on a licensing system originally set up for fire safety reasons, a device which conveniently avoided direct machinery for censorship. Likewise in 1978 the British Labour government looked for instruments with which to control pay increases. Purpose-built tools could not be used at that time, because pay control was opposed by the labour unions and by a large part of the Labour party itself. So the government tried to use instruments designed for other purposes, such as government contracts and grants, or export credit guarantees, which could be denied to employers conceding high wage rises to their workers.

The formal constraints imposed by international institutions also give governments very powerful incentives for searching surreptitiously for instruments to use out of context in pursuit of aims that cannot be acknowledged openly. The European Common Market is a fertile source of examples showing the ingenuity that governments can display in pursuing trade protection policies by instruments designed for other purposes. The Federal German government has used sixteenth-century quality control regulations to shut its beer market to other members of the 'Common' Market (*Die Zeit*, 12 March 1982). The British government for a time used the vehicle registration system to block its subjects from importing new cars bought in other EEC countries at prices lower than those prevailing in Britain (*The Sunday Times*, 18 October 1981).

In such circumstances 'rummaging' can turn into tit-for-tat competition among governments. The Anglo-French 'turkey war' of 1981 is a case in point. At that time the British Conservative government was under political pressure to protect its poultry farmers from cheap French turkey imports. Given that the EEC, to which both countries belonged, maintains a (supposedly) free market in agricultural produce, the British government had to find instruments designed for some purpose other than trade protection. Accordingly it chose to revert from the then current practice of vaccinating British turkeys against fowl pest to the pre-1963 system by which government slaughtered all turkeys in which the disease was confirmed by its own vets and compensated the owner for his loss. This meant, of course, that the British government could conveniently refuse to accept poultry imports from countries still using vaccination as the chosen instrument for disease control, as was the case in France. But this card did not long remain an ace, because the French government *also* promptly changed from a vaccination to a slaughter approach to fowl pest. The point is, of course, that neither move was prompted in reality by concern about animal disease, to which the instruments involved are ostensibly directed.

Government may commonly fail to choose consciously among its instruments when designing policy programmes, as Mayntz (1981) complains. But that is not always the case. Government rummages through its tool-set more commonly than one might think – often for devious reasons. And the pressures that lead governments to behave in this way are not likely to abate.

Comparative analysis

Seeing government as a tool-kit can also prompt us to draw comparisons and contrasts between different kinds of government activity, even though those activities may be in disparate policy areas or taking place at different points in space or time. Previous chapters touched on this point when discussing each of the main classes of government instrument. But the total picture deserves a little discussion.

Government tools or tools of government?

One kind of comparative question that may already have occurred to the reader is: what is so special about *government's* tools? Are they qualitatively different from those used in the world outside government, and so amounting to some sort of specialised 'government technology'?

In many ways the answer is no. Many, perhaps most, of the tools used by government are not in any way special or unique. As we saw in Part I, government's attempts to make an impact on the world outside do not, much of the time, differ from those of other organisations in terms of the basic tools of the trade. Government is not using especially unusual tools when it seeks to persuade or to propagandise, when it buys or sells or gives money away. Government's tokens of authority, as we saw in Chapter 4, have parallels in many cases with instruments used by organisations outside government. Private or independent organisations issue certificates, franchises, licences and guarantees. Again, much of government's direct or physical operations on the world at large and its means of obtaining information have parallels with instruments used by other organisations. Even quite specific activities which one might think of as peculiarly 'government-like', such as the minting of coinage or the provision of lighthouses, have private-sector parallels (see Binney, 1958, p. 31).

Some government tools, on the other hand, *are* certainly special: they are specifically government tools rather than common-or-garden instruments that happen to be used by government. Government's requisitions for obtaining information from the world outside (other than as a contractual condition or within the confines of an organisation) are one case in point. So are government's official tokens in the form of orders and prohibitions of a 'general' type. These are not really paralleled by trade union 'licences to work' and the like.

Moreover, there are differences, not so much in the basic instruments used as in the emphasis and the specific application, especially when it comes to 'treatment'. For example, many other organisations provide custodial treatment, but there are no non-government organisations running prisons or institutions for the criminally insane. And government may apply its instruments on a scale and range that is unique. For example, a criminal organisation may well illegally use government-like instruments ('contracts' by 'hit men', detention by kidnappers), but only an extraordinarily sophisticated one – indeed, one which was practically a government in its own right – could match government's range.

Tools of which government?

Of course, comparing the tools used by 'government' with those of non-government organisations can only be done at a very general level. The result depends to a large extent on which government we are speaking of, or even which part of which level of government. Once we start to disaggregate government – that is, to distinguish separate pieces and levels – our minds begin to turn to other kinds of comparisons.

For example, it is rare to find the full range of government tools being deployed at the extreme 'ends' of government. At the most parochial level of government (the village committee, etc.), the instruments in use may not amount to much more than information-dispensers, relying mainly on nodality and with little or no use of instruments based on treasure, authority and organisation. At the other end of the scale, institutions of international 'government' are also typically very limited in the tools they can use. Even the European Economic Community, which has some pretensions to being a relatively strong 'supranational' government institution, has very little in the way of 'organisation' at its disposal. It has to rely on nodality, treasure and authority, and even then it does not make use of some of the important instruments based on those resources, such as propaganda.

It is in between these two ends of the scale, at central and intermediate levels of government, that we are likely to find most or all of the tools in the bag in use. Differences here are likely to be more a matter of emphasis or of application, more of sub-categories than of the main classes of government tools. Moreover, the 'spread' or the range of differences among the patterns of tools in use varies widely from agency to agency or from department to department at any level of government. For example, in Britain the Ministry of Defence uses practically every tool in the bag, from publishing magazines for would-be soldiers to physical bombardment and alterations to the landscape, whereas central education departments are limited to a narrow range of money-moving tools and tokens of authority. If the 'spread' at each level turns out to be as great as the overall differences between levels, we might want to disaggregate the comparison still further, to the level of individual government agencies.

Comparing government agencies

Table 7.1 illustrates how the main classes of government tools discussed in this book might be applied by three fictional government agencies with different purposes. When we start comparing government agencies with one another in these terms, two points emerge.

First, in spite of the different substantive tasks and policies of each agency, some of government's tools keep popping up, so to speak, in different contexts. The mix and the applications certainly differ, but government's tools are no respecters of administrative boundaries – as we would expect, given the point (made in Chapter 1) that governments tend to organise themselves according to purposes rather than instruments. It is true that not all of the agencies in Table 7.1 use instruments based on treasure or organisation for both effecting and detecting. But it is a rare government agency that makes no use whatever of instruments based on nodality and authority. All three agencies in Table 7.1 rely heavily on 'authority', both for effecting and detecting.

Second, the emphasis, mix and context of application varies from case to case, and comparing government agencies in terms of their tool-kit is one way of bringing out what is distinctive or otherwise about the 'production function' of any given agency. For the three agencies shown in Table 7.1, Agency A, as is characteristic of many agricultural agencies, would probably put roughly equal weight on each of the four 'pillars' of the 'NATO' scheme, making for an unusually broad-based 'mix'. Agencies B and C, by contrast, would probably put the heaviest weight on authority-based instruments and less on the other three. When it comes to the use of organisation-based instruments, Agencies A and B show opposite patterns. A uses organisation for effectors but not detectors, B for detectors but not effectors; C uses it for both effectors *and* detectors.

Of course, making comparisons at an 'agency-wide' level still involves a fairly high level of aggregation. One can get a different picture if one takes the next step and looks at the constituent units within agencies. For example, suppose that Agency C in Table 7.1 – the tax-collection agency – was divided into a section dealing with customs duties and a section dealing with all other taxes. The tool-using differences between the two sections might then be just as marked as those between the three separate agencies. We could expect the customs section, in the nature of its work, to make much heavier use of organisation, both for effecting and detecting, than the other section. Customs detection typically makes significant use of the whole battery of 'ergonomic detectors', using turnstiles, fixed, mobile and hidden scanners to a considerable degree. Such devices would be unlikely to be so heavily used by the other section. We could also expect direct action to figure much larger in the 'effecting' operations of the customs section than in those of the other section, with the much greater emphasis typically involved in

TABLE 7.1 Applying government's tools: three (fictional) government agencies

Instruments used: some examples of applications	AGENCY A Agricultural services	AGENCY B Services to trade and commerce	AGENCY C Tax collection
(1) Nodality-based instruments			
Effectors	Advice to farmers	Advice to exporters; trade promotion	Tax reminders
Detectors	Agricultural surveys	Receipt of complaints about unfair trading	Receipt of malevolent information on tax evasion
(2) Treasure-based instruments			
Effectors	Grants, loans, subsidies to farmers	Grants to organisations for trade promotion, etc.	
Detectors	Information from applications	Use of consultancy services	Paid tax informers
(3) Authority-based instruments			
Effectors	Certification of healthy stock; import and export licenses;	Certification of successful export companies; import and export	Clearances for customs and probate certificates; licences for excise

	prohibitions of animal movements (disease control); orders to destroy weeds	licences; grant of patents; tariff orders	traders; tax assessments; tax amnesties
Detectors	Registration of farms; notification of animal diseases; farm inspections	Registration of companies, trade marks, hall marks; investigations of bankruptcy	Tax declarations and returns; registration of taxable traders (for sales and excise taxes); tax inspections and raids
(4) **Organisation-based instruments**			
Effectors	Marking of subsidised animals; stud farms and artificial insemination centres; vaccination and slaughter of farm animals; destruction of pests; plant and animal quarantine	–	Stamping of legal documents (for stamp taxes); marking of spirits; bonded stores; arrest and seizure operations.
Detectors	–	Coastguard	Traffic scrutiny at ports and airports

customs work on direct pursuit and seizure, on processes of sealing and marking and bonded stores. Most other kinds of tax operations the province of the other section in this imaginary agency make authority relatively more important, both for detecting and effecting.

The 'cells' of government institutions could, of course, be split into progressively smaller sub-units, and indeed, the results of organisational comparison are often highly sensitive to the choice of the level or unit to be compared. The point here, however, is not to develop that question but simply to show the kind of lines that comparisons in terms of the 'tool-kit' can follow.

Re-tooling: change over time

One of the other familiar problems in comparing organisations is that they rarely stand still. So to 'stop the clock' and compare at a single point in time often produces an unrealistic result, like an uncharacteristic or trick photograph depicting only one part of a sequence. But the sequence itself may be just as interesting. Often we want to compare over time as well as cross-sectionally. Looking back to observe the various instruments employed by governments from time to time to tackle some problem or other can have the same fascination for the student of government administration that the engineer gets from early cars or bicycles.

One fairly common type of transition runs from reliance on nodality alone to instruments based on other resources (see Lowi, 1969). Governments may move from military recruitment propaganda to conscription, from exhortations to save fuel to fuel rationing, from persuasion to force. For example, one of the British government's first moves in the Anglo-Icelandic fishing conflicts of the late 1960s and early 1970s was to set up an 'advice centre' in the form of a government support ship to act as an information exchange for British trawlers fishing off Iceland. Similarly, the first step taken by the British government to abandon the traditional principle of free trade in the 1920s was the propagation of publicity (through the Empire Marketing Board of 1923–33) to encourage its subjects to prefer home and imperial produce to that from other sources. The next step, in 1931, was from the information-dispenser to the official token, in the form of the Imperial Tariff (Ogilvy-Webb, 1965, pp. 52–3). After Britain entered the free-trade zone of the European Community in 1973, 'buy British' propaganda became more important again.

Another fairly common type of transition runs from reliance on authority alone to the use of treasure or organisation. For example, when government in Britain began to interest itself in preventing the spread of cattle plague, the first step was to deploy official tokens, ordering farmers and landowners to slaughter diseased stock when the occasion arose. Late in the nineteenth century, government moved into the business of slaughtering diseased animals itself and compensating the owner for the loss (Winnifrith, 1962).

Similarly, an early attempt to tackle the problem of overcrowding in the slum tenements of Glasgow relied solely on authority, in the form of official quotas which specified the maximum number of people permitted by government to inhabit each house (Mitchison, 1970, pp. 403–4). Detection was by periodic police inspections, during which the 'surplus' population of each house took refuge among the chimney-stacks, just as surplus passengers dismount when overloaded buses approach police check-points in some of the poorer countries of the present day. Modern British approaches to the 'overcrowded housing' problem supplement official quotas by a battery of cheque-book measures and of direct action in the form of physical provision of houses.

In other cases governments may turn from one instrument to another without much evidence of a 'linear' progression, either because the 'problem' is stubborn to attack (crime control, promotion of economic development) or because the context is highly contentious, or both. It is like trying to modify a child's behaviour by switching the emphasis from reasoning to peremptory commands, bribes or physical coercion without settling on any of these methods for long.

British government approaches to the labour unions in the 1970s and early 1980s might be taken as an example of this kind of instrument switching. In the attempt to hold down union pay increases, governments of both major parties have switched among open compacts, group-conduited forms of conditional tokens, constraints, direct action in the form of strike-breaking by government troops taking over fire services or refuse collection, 'rummage bag' (as in the example given earlier of the 1978 search for under-the-counter ways of hitting employers who conceded 'over-large' pay rises), and nothing at all.

Specifically Conservative governments in Britain during this period have also tried to influence trade union structure more directly. But they too have switched among different instruments for this purpose.

For example, the Conservative government of the early 1970s tried unsuccessfully to control union behaviour by a system of 'enablements', e.g. government licensing of unions and bestowing 'privileges' while also imposing legal responsibilities. In practice, most unions handed their government licences back (Thomson and Engleman, 1975, Barnes and Reid, 1980) and this approach was not taken up again by the Conservative government of 1979. Again, the Conservatives in the earlier period tried to control union strike decisions by constraints, in the form of government orders to unions to hold ballots over strikes or to delay strike action for a given period – 'cooling off' procedures closely modelled on US practice. The 1979 Conservative government (perhaps because of the chastening experience of its predecessor in trying to use such orders) switched to cheque-book tactics instead, simply offering government money for unions to take up if they wished for the purpose of holding secret ballots of their members.

This is a slightly different case from the examples given earlier. Here government is switching among its repertoire to find the tool for the job, in a situation of high conflict with the 'target group' to which its activities are directed. But the need to keep an 'enemy' guessing is not, of course, the only reason for switching or oscillating from one government instrument to another. Frequently there are dilemmas involved in the choice of instruments by government (Hood, 1976; Dunsire, 1978). Using one instrument may well bring about undesirable side-effects; but the alternatives may be similarly attended by unwanted by-products. The more active government becomes, the more manifestations of such dilemmas may develop. This is one of the reasons for the growth of interest in 'policy succession'.

Policy succession – or nothing new under the sun?

It is not an accident that there should be widespread interest in charting the way government changes its approach to policy problems over time, turning from one instrument to another. The phenomenon has been termed by Peters and Hogwood (1980) as 'policy succession', to distinguish it from the entry of government into completely new social territory or, conversely, the total departure of government from some field of activity.

Peters and Hogwood argue plausibly that as government activities have come to embrace more and more aspects of social life, there is less virgin territory for government to move in to. This is a theme that was mentioned in Chapter 1. With the 'ending of the frontier', so to speak, government's 'policy space' becomes crowded with agencies and programmes. Hence, argue Peters and Hogwood, government in the future is likely to be increasingly concerned with policy succession. It will be trying to react to the dilemmas created by unwanted or unanticipated side-effects arising from the use of government instruments in an ever more crowded policy space (Offe, 1975, pp. 88–9; Wildavsky, 1980). It will be searching for new packages of instruments to apply to areas where the set of instruments originally chosen does not seem to answer the purpose.

Of course, the discussion of government's tool-kit in this book may make us wary of the idea that there can be such a thing as a 'new' government instrument. There is nothing new under the sun. As has already been stressed, most of the instruments used by government are generic types, having a long ancestry. But, as we have also seen, it is in a sense *both* true that there is nothing new under the sun *and* that there is vast scope for innovation in the use of government's instruments.

This is not so much of a paradox as it might seem. Provided there is a mechanism for generating variants – mutations or innovations – complex evolutionary processes can operate on the basis of a relatively fixed population of basic types. The interesting question, of course, is what *are* the mechanisms for generating innovation in this case? It can be suggested that when novelty is generated in government instruments, one or all of three things may be happening.

First, an old instrument may be applied in a new *context*. This happens all the time, often through a process of imitation (Simon, Smithburg and Thompson, 1950, p. 38; Nelson and Winter, 1982). As we saw in Chapter 4, government is forever wheeling out old stand-bys such as compulsory registration or licensing schemes in new contexts. Imperial licences for the operation of printing presses are translated into the present-day system of government licensing of broadcasting stations (Enzensberger, 1970, p. 13). Procedures for closing canals are translated into procedures for closing railway lines (Dunsire, 1978, p. 93). Procedures for government control over railways are translated into procedures for government control over aviation (Breyer (1982, p. 6) shows that the 1938 US Civil Aeronautics Act was indirectly modelled on the 1845 British Railway Act.) Very simple applications of authority, such as traditional 'tall chimney' requirements as a means of controlling pollution, may be replaced by more complex applications to cope with an era of 'acid rain' and the like (Knoepfel and Wiedner, in Mayntz, 1980, p. 97).

Sometimes the step taken by government is a bit bigger than these examples indicate, but the principle is the same. For example, before 1896 the British government had no machinery for routine involvement in conciliating labour–management disputes, a process which is essentially an application of nodality both as detector and effector. *Ad hoc* applications of nodality for such purposes occasionally took place, such as the Foreign Office's involvement in a major coal strike in 1893, an event which had strategic implications for a naval power relying on coal-fired steamships (Wigham, 1976). When the government decided to equip itself for such activity on a regular basis, it modelled the machinery on an 1888 system for government conciliation of disputes over railway freight rates between clients and carriers. There was nothing new about the mix of instruments employed. It was only the context that was new. The original railway freight rates system is long since defunct and forgotten, while conciliation of labour disputes has become a commonplace of modern government's activities (Llewellyn Smith, 1928, p. 141).

Second, an old instrument may change in salience as a result of technological change. For example, in government detection, the 'ear of Dionysus' of classical times and government's traditional monopoly of the carriage of mails (enabling it secretly to read its subjects' letters) have been tranformed by technological change into the electronic hidden scanners of our own day: lie detectors, 'bugs', radar speed traps, etc. In the case of information-dispensers, the development of computerised records makes some kinds of direct notifications (such as reminders tailored to individuals) less expensive for government than would be the case if government had to use old-fashioned manual methods. Even treatment may change in character as a result of technological change. At one time, madmen and some of government's more implacable enemies had to be kept in chains or cages, there being little in the way of alternative instruments open to government apart from torture or execution. Modern government still uses incarceration on a large scale, but it has a wider range of possible alternative treatments at its disposal, such as frontal lobotomy or the administration of behaviour-modifying drugs.

Third, novelty may mean a *combination* or *mix* of instruments different from what existed before. The ingredients are the same but the recipe is different. It is very common, as we have already seen, to find government shifting the balance from one tool to another without abandoning any of them completely. An example might be the constantly changing balance of information-dispensing, tokens of authority (including tax exemptions) and money moving that governments deploy in the hope of directing business investment.

Thus, even with an unchanging repertoire of basic instruments, a powerful potential for generating novelty is afforded by context, combination and technological form. Of course, it may take a certain touch of 'administrative genius' to realise this potential – to spot a 'niche' or a new combination or to see how an instrument can be carried over from one context to another. Not everyone can do it in practice. But at least the process can be understood.

Conclusion

This chapter has suggested some of the ways in which seeing government activities as the application of a set of tools can alter our thinking about government. It can enable us to reduce variety, to generate variety, to think in terms of alternative ways of doing things rather than in conventional or traditional grooves, and to compare government activities, both cross-sectionally and over time.

The discussion of changes over time has been restricted to the level of individual 'problems', such as labour disputes and fisheries. There is, of course, also a macro or government-wide level at which such changes can take place. That is, we can look at the profile of instruments deployed by government as a whole and examine how that aggregate profile may change over time. 'Policy succession' at this very general level is discussed in the final chapter.

There is a further element so far missing from the discussion. Many readers will be wondering how government is to decide whether any tool is good or bad for some specific purpose. Previous chapters have skirted round this issue. Effective choice, as was mentioned earlier, requires that we have an idea of the range of alternative instruments that might conceivably be brought into play in some case or another. But it requires somewhat more than that, of course. It requires the ability to pick tools that will do a given job *satisfactorily*. But what does 'satisfactorily' mean? The next chapter picks up this theme and explores possible criteria by which we might appraise the use of government's instruments.

8 Appraising Government's Tools

It's a poor workman who blames his tools.

(old saw)

Up till now we have looked at government's tools with a dispassionate eye. We have sought to analyse and understand, not to judge or evaluate. We have noticed the diversity of ways in which government uses its set of tools in different contexts; the many possible combinations that the set is capable of generating, and the ways in which the pattern can change over time as government tries to find the right tools for a job. It is now time to address ourselves more directly to the question of what makes a *good* choice of tools.

This is another of those 'plain man's questions' that can lead us into very deep waters. Tools can be good or bad in at least two possible senses. Good might mean morally right; or it might be used in a purely engineering sense of efficiency and effectiveness. A tool can be said to be good if it does the job required of it.

Whichever sense of 'good' we want to use, we still have to find some way of distinguishing the good from the bad. Most of the time, in seeing a choice of instruments by government as inept or inspired, we judge case by case, *ex post*, on the basis of common sense. Such judgements, based on hindsight and applied to the experience of some specific venture, are the stock-in-trade of the administrative historian. But there is no elaborate science in this: it is like knowing an elephant when we see one. Context is everything. If this is the only method of appraisal open to us, it means that we can only look at applications of government instruments one by one, after the event, by a minute examination of the context and circumstances of each case.

We might be content with that. Alternatively, we might try – more ambitiously but more dangerously – to lay out a set of explicit principles by which good or bad applications might be judged. Is it possible to propose a set of 'canons' for the use of government's administrative tools, like the four famous 'canons of taxation' laid down in 1776 by the economist Adam Smith (1910, pp. 307–8)? That is the question to which this chapter is addressed.

Some possible canons

In this chapter, four canons of 'good application' of government instruments are explored. Many other possible criteria could, of course, be added. But the four taken here should suffice to give an idea of the difficulties of appraisal.

It might be held that a good application of government instruments would satisfy the following criteria:

(1) The instrument or mix of instruments used in any given case should be selected after some examination of alternative possible tools for the job.
(2) The tool should be matched to the job. Since there is no general purpose tool that will serve government effectively in all circumstances, government needs to understand the circumstances which favour each of the instruments available.
(3) The choice must not be 'barbaric'; it must satisfy certain ethical criteria, such as justice and fairness.
(4) Effectiveness is not enough; the desired effect must be achieved with the minimum possible drain on government's bureaucratic resources.

These are very simple, commonsense canons. But, as will be seen, each of them presents considerable difficulty when it is applied in practice. Moreover, they belong together. Each canon depends upon and in some cases limits the others. If government does not have any sense of what alternatives are available for any job, it is unlikely to know what circumstances favour which instruments. If it does not know the latter, it has no basis for choosing tools that will be effective, except on the basis of blind trial and error. And if this condition is not met, government has in turn no basis for achieving economy – a choice of tools that will be effective with minimum deployment of effort. Again, any idea of bringing ethical criteria to bear presupposes that there *is* some choice to be made: in other words, that alternatives can be identified.

And if government does not make its choices within certain ethical parameters, there ceases to be any defensible reason for wanting government's tools to be applied effectively or economically. On the contrary. we may positively welcome ineffectiveness and waste of resources in those circumstances.

Interdependent as they are, these canons will now be separated out and discussed in the order they are set out above. The first three will be discussed fairly briefly, but the fourth – the idea of 'using bureaucracy sparingly' – will be explored in a little more depth.

Reviewing alternatives: a rational choice?

One possible criterion by which we might judge the selection of administrative instruments is to look at the procedure by which the choice is made.

Now we may, by luck or intuition, make a brilliantly successful choice by trusting a hunch, or by any one of a hundred arbitrary methods of making a snap decision. But that is not a *rational* way to choose.

A chooser must adopt a quite different approach if the choice is to qualify as 'rational'. Formally, he or she must: (a) specify the goal(s) to be reached; (b) identify all the possible ways or means by which the goal might be reached; (c) ascertain the likely consequences of each alternative; and (d) choose the alternative that is likely to reach the goal(s) with the greatest certainty, to the greatest extent, or with the minimum of effort.

Having thus baldly stated the canons of rational choice, we immediately encounter all sorts of theoretical puzzles. These puzzles are familiar in the literature on the subject. At what point, for example, does the chooser decide that the costs of extra search for information about alternatives are likely to outweigh the advantages of making a better choice as a result of further search? How is risk and uncertainty to be accommodated? This is crucial, for to the extent that there is less than perfect certainty in the information available to the chooser, a choice may turn out to be disastrously wrong in practice, even if it faithfully follows the procedure of examining all the feasible alternatives that seem to be available.

In spite of these very familiar problems, the conception of rational choice does at least serve to offer one *procedural* criterion for a good choice. Can this computer-chess formula for decision be applied to the choice of government's administrative tools? Up to a point, yes; but only up to a point.

As was pointed out in the last chapter, looking through a simple inventory of government tools such as that discussed earlier in the book may serve as a guide for noticing the different types of instrument that might be available for tackling any given problem. And certainly, one might expect any able government official to be capable of ranging freely and automatically among the contents of the administrative tool-box, either by intuition or from long experience. High public officials, after all, are supposed to be the master mechanics of government's machine; and they are expected to be capable of choosing with some show of rationality, presenting and discussing alternatives and choosing the tool for the job after due deliberation, so that the process can at least be defended after the event.

In reality, it is common knowledge that choice normally falls far short of this procedural standard. Perhaps one could say that a choice which at least seriously considers some alternatives is *more* rational than a choice which plumps for one instrument without even considering the possibility that there might be other ways of going about the job. But choosing among government's instruments cannot be a fully rational process, even in theory.

This is because, as we saw in Chapter 7, the number of alternative combinations of government instruments, even on the very simplified scheme presented in this book, runs into billions or even trillions if one assumes no incompatibilities or mutual exclusivities. So, however desirable it might seem, any strict application of rational-choice procedure is simply impossible in this case. No one, in any finite time, can consider systematically so large a number of alternatives in any specific context.

It follows, then, that government cannot examine *all* feasible alternatives in most cases. The choice in practice merely lies between examining a greater or smaller number of combinations of instruments, depending on the circumstances. Certainly, one might expect the search to intensify when government perceives itself to have failed in tackling some problem. But even in that case, the choice of the tool for the job must in practice rest largely on intuition, experience, tradition, faith and serendipity. We saw an example of serendipity in Chapter 7, when we noticed that the British railway rates conciliation system was conceived as a device that could be applied to labour–management relations simply because, by the accident of history, in the late nineteenth century the same department of government happened to be responsible both for railways and for industrial relations. Administrative history abounds with cases of this type.

Instrument choice as politics

Given that all feasible alternatives cannot be systematically appraised, it follows that in many cases *politics* will play a large part in the selection of tools for the job. The idea of government cooly and open-mindedly browsing round its tool-shed to select the most effective instrument for the job in hand – the image with which we began in Chapter 1 – is, of course, quite unrealistic. Just as some weapons may be eschewed in war for high strategic or political reasons, so there are typically political or ideological constraints on the use of some of the instruments in government's tool-shed to attack domestic policy problems. Governments will use massive police swoops for fiscal or public-order purposes, but not to enforce such things as safety at work laws. Labour governments in Britain will tend to avoid using policy instruments on labour unions that involve ordering, forbidding or even licensing. As Schaffer and Lamb (1981, p. 7) put it, 'search for alternatives . . . is neither random nor open-minded'.

Indeed, very commonly it is the instrument selected for realising a policy aim that is far more contentious than the aim itself. This was touched upon in Chapter 1. For example, few would argue that it is completely wrong for government to take measures to prevent diseases. Government in Britain has been seriously engaged in trying to prevent the spread of cattle disease since the eighteenth century, and extended its concern to human diseases in the nineteenth century. But by what instruments should government pursue this laudable goal? Should it systematically exterminate potentially disease-carrying wild animals such as badgers? Should it conduct intimate medical examinations of everyone entering the country? Should it operate its own brothels (as governments do in some countries) as a means of trying to check sexually transmitted diseases? Should it add chemicals to the water supply?

Questions such as these are 'hot politics', linked to complex and often unstated assumptions about the cases and effects of social phenomena, as with the familiar argument about 'tough' versus 'soft' treatment of criminals. The simplistic idea that 'politics' is about 'the big picture', the broad aims or major goals, and that the 'delivery' or implementation of these goals is a non-political task for technocrats or administrators, is often the exact opposite of the truth. Commonly, the real politics only *begins* when it comes to the choice of implements.

Matching the tool to the job

Effective choice requires more than a review of alternatives, to the extent that such a review is possible. It also requires some understanding of how to match instruments to circumstances. We have a range of tools precisely because in some circumstances we use one tool, in other circumstances we use another. In difficult marginal cases it may be a nice question where one tool is more suitable than another. Experts may disagree. But we certainly cannot use our tools randomly, as a child might do, with much hope of success.

What are the contexts in which specific government tools perform well or badly? Working assumptions and rules of thumb are constantly used in the workshop of government bureaucracy; each agency has its own store of experience and pragmatic folk-wisdom about what works in its own specific area. But the lore is not written down; and, since it is rarely made explicit, its reliability is hard to test.

One attempt to spell things out a little has been made by Renate Mayntz (1981). She compares the selection of policy instruments by government to the selection of structures in organisations. What is nowadays known as 'contingency theory' (Kast and Rosenzweig, 1973) grew up in the 1960s as an attempt to specify what types of organisational structures are likely to be found in which contexts, once it had been recognised that there was no single blueprint for the 'best' organisational structure in any circumstances. In the same way, Mayntz believes, theory can develop for matching government instruments to policy contexts, given that there is no single policy instrument that is ideal in all circumstances.

This is a bold and imaginative idea. One could not, of course, imagine that it will ever be possible to specify such contingencies completely, for exactly the same reason that it is impossible to review all the alternatives that might be deployed in combination. There is too much potential variety. Most government selection of its instruments must be like natural selection in evolution – a mixture of chance and trial and error. But 'better sma' fish than nane', and some possible links deserve examination.

Mayntz discusses four, in a very tentative way. She suggests that where government is dealing with networks of organisations (rather than working in fields where there are few or no large organisations), it will tend to rely more on persuasion, cheque-book and general standard-setting rather than on direct action or on other types of official token. Second, echoing an observation that goes back to David Hume, she suggests that tokens of authority of the ordering or forbidding type will be inadequate where the aim is to achieve some voluntary effort on the part of government's subjects and not just grudging compliance. However – this is Mayntz's third point – where government's aim is to redistribute income, wealth or access to other resources within society, it will require 'hard' regulatory instruments. What 'hard' regulatory instruments are is not precisely set out by Mayntz, but presumably it means constraints and enablements rather than certificates, direct action rather than money-moving or propaganda, requisitions and ergonomic detectors rather than nodal receivers or rewards. Fourth, where government is already deploying a multiplicity of instruments in some specific context, the addition of others may have diminishing, nil or negative results owing to mutual self-cancellation and/or diminishing returns.

Pressing Mayntz's analogy with contingency theory in organisational analysis a little further, it is worth noticing that the three main predictors of organisational structure that have been established by contingency theories are size of organisation, environment and technology. Of these, by far the most powerful is size. The effects of environment and technology are much less clear-cut and universal, partly because they are very difficult to conceptualise and measure in a way that can be applied to all organisations.

In the somewhat different context of government instruments, size also seems to be important. One theme running through all the chapters in Parts I and II of this book was the effect of size, not of organisation but of clientele, as an important influence on the type of policy instruments likely to be selected. It was suggested that, by and large, the larger this population is, the more government is likely to want to switch the balance of emphasis from active to passive instruments or from particular to general ones. In the latter case, a very common load-shedding device is to concentrate on intermediaries or 'conduits' in matters such as cheque-book operations, information or even official tokens.

'Environment' is also an important influence. Another thread running through the earlier chapters was the effect of increasing pressure on government, in the sense of lack of consensus or disaffection among its subjects, concerning the mix of instruments employed. The 'goal' congruence or otherwise that exists among government and its subjects has a major impact on the type and mix of tools in use, and this will be discussed further in the next chapter.

Other large-scale 'contingencies' are not so clear. Technology in this case is not so much a predictor as what has to be explained. As we saw in Chapter 7, changes in machine technology may affect the salience of a government tool, but in an important sense government's 'technology' *is* the mix of administrative instruments that it uses. Evidently, much more needs to be done in divining the contingencies governing the use of its instruments before government can be equipped with the systematic knowledge of how to 'match the tool to the job' which it would need to fulfil the second 'canon' for applying its instruments well.

A moral dimension?

Part of the reason for the 'hot politics' dimension of selecting government tools is the *uncertainty* of the link between wish and fulfilment in many areas of government activity. Improving health, reducing crime and increasing economic prosperity: these are only three obvious cases in which the instruments that are appropriate for delivering the desired result are highly uncertain and disputed.

The 'politicisation' of government's selection of tools highlights the moral dimension involved in that choice. Are there ethical criteria which any choice of tools must satisfy? This is the third possible canon that was sketched out earlier.

Such a canon is in fact just as problematic as all the others. It is easy enough to argue, as does Hodgkinson (1978, p. 65), that administrators should be unusually sensitive to ethical questions; it would be difficult to argue the opposite. But to *what* values exactly should government be sensitive? Modern writers on ethics have to face up to the fact that many societies contain a variety of different and competing moral codes, not a single over-arching one. In those circumstances, many such writers are forced into advancing canons for moral choice that are purely procedural (van Gunsteren, 1981, p. 6) – and that includes Hodgkinson, too (1978, p. 220). What that means in practice is the adoption of 'responsible' procedures and attitudes when making a choice. In this context, that comes close to the rational choice canon and leads to exactly the same difficulties.

Nor is that the only difficulty. Are moral judgements to be applied to instruments themselves or only to the *applications* of such instruments? This book began by making a simple comparison between government's administrative instruments and a set of garden tools, or a carpentry set. Plainly, it would be absurd to seek to apply moral judgements to the latter, separating 'evil' instruments from 'good' ones. But does the same apply to the former? Are government's tools 'mere' instruments?

In one sense one may confidently say that there is no such thing as good or bad tools, only good or bad purposes. The axe that one man might use to cut down a dangerous tree or to rescue victims trapped in a fire might be used by another to hack some innocent person to pieces. Good or evil lies in the purpose or application, not the instrument.

But does this apply equally to *government's* tools? Some would argue the tough-minded case that government's tools *are* exactly like garden tools in this sense. They are evil only when they are used by the other side (so to speak) or for the wrong political purposes. By implication this is the position of every group of revolutionaries which, on coming to power, employs the very instruments of coercion that, in the hands of the old regime, attracted the group's moral condemnation.

Against that, there is a widespread feeling, regularly expressed in political argument and behaviour, that some government instruments *are* intrinsically more acceptable than others. Some weapons of warfare, for example, have been singled out as especially 'immoral' by critics, from the longbow in the Middle Ages to the machine-gun in 1914 and the atomic bomb of our own times. Indeed, all the instruments we looked at in Parts I and II raise keen moral questions. Direct action tools and propaganda are obvious cases; and detection similarly raises questions such as those relating to the 'right to privacy' (Cornford, 1981) and to the ethics of hydra-headed government snooping into our affairs. Denunciations of such government tools are a commonplace of modern political argument.

There are two well known difficulties with this kind of approach. One is that there is no such thing as an intrinsically 'innocent' instrument of government. It might seem plausible to suggest that a 'civilised' government would, wherever possible, prefer tools that involve low constraint on individuals to those involving high constraint (preferring, for example, propaganda to treatment, certification to constraint, money-moving to direct action, nodal receivers and rewards to requisitions and ergonomic detectors). But this does not really solve the problem. We have to face up to the possbility of unpleasant applications even of low-constraint instruments, for example propagandising young children or using 'ear trumpet' methods to encourage busybodies to tell government's secret police about ideological deviations on the part of their relatives or neighbours. No government instruments are inherently 'clean'. Deny government those instruments that might be applied barbarically, and you deny it almost the whole tool-box.

The other difficulty is the age-old argument that government may sometimes, even frequently, be obliged to use 'the instruments of evil to do good', as Ostrom (1982) puts it; and this can apply even if we do not see government's tool-box as ethically neutral, like garden tools. This is the 'dirty hands', teleological-deontological dilemma that has been discussed by political theorists since St Augustine and Machiavelli (van Gunsteren, 1981, p. 6; Kagan, 1978, p. 9): what if unpleasant instruments produce beneficial results? Or the reverse, as with the standard argument that outlawing the most powerful weapons of warfare only serves to make wars more frequent, less controllable and more prolonged?

No one would deny that the use of government's tools, even for everyday purposes, is shot through with moral problems and choices, and that any appraisal of the use of these tools must include this dimension (Hodgkinson, 1978). But there is no simple rule of thumb that can be applied here. Each case has to be argued on its merits.

Economy: using bureaucracy sparingly

A fourth possible criterion for judging a 'good' selection of government tools is that of *economy*. This has already been touched upon in several chapters. 'Economy' is, of course, one of Adam Smith's canons of taxation and a long-standing 'principle' of government administration in general (see Simon, Smithburg and Thompson, 1950, p. 60; Hodgkinson, 1978, p. 210).

There is a saying in the horse-racing community that 'a good big 'un is better than a good little 'un'. We could almost say that the opposite applies to government administrative tools. The real test of administrative engineering is to achieve the effect desired with the very minimum of bureaucratic building materials. Using bureaucracy sparingly, i.e. making a little of it go a long way, is the acme of the bureaucrat's craft. Anyone can make a house stand up if, as our ancestors did, they build the walls several feet thick. But this is grossly wasteful of labour, materials and space. It takes the professional skills of the architect or of the trained builder to construct a strong building with the minimum of materials. Similarly, it is not sufficient for government to find tools that are effective, in the sense that they do the job required of them. Strictly, to do a good job, the tools must also be efficient, performing the task in the most economical way.

However, the idea of 'using bureaucracy sparingly' has more than one possible meaning. It could mean at least two possible things:

(a) minimising the effort, expense and manpower needed by government to undertake a certain task; and
(b) visiting on the people at large no more 'trouble, vexation and oppression' (in Adam Smith's phrase – 1910, p. 309) than is absolutely necessary to achieve the aim in view.

These two possible ways of using bureaucracy sparingly by no means always lead in the same direction, as we will see in the following sections.

Minimising government's effort, expense and manpower

'Saving on bureaucracy' in the first sense mentioned above will tend to lead government to prefer general to particular effectors and passive to active detectors. In a wider sense it may lead government to prefer to base its operations on what will be termed 'contingently' rather than 'immanently' depletable resources.

Preferring general to particular effectors and passive to active detectors as ways of saving on bureaucracy will be familiar to the reader from the discussion in earlier chapters. But it is important to note that the 'bureaucracy-saving' involved here is a *total* or *absolute* one. If what government wants to do is save on bureaucracy *per unit of output* (rather than keeping the total bureaucracy down to a minimum), it might well be led in the opposite direction in circumstances where additions to the total bureaucracy might have more than proportionate effects on revenue, demand or output. But the analytic complications this introduces are too great to be handled here; this discussion is limited to 'using bureaucracy sparingly' only in an absolute sense.

In that sense, as we have seen, particular effectors are typically bureaucracy-intensive weapons in terms of the discrimination effort they involve, and government is often drawn to the use of general types or group 'conduits' as load-shedding devices, applying the ancient principle of tax-farming to new contexts.

For example, when government in Britain introduced annual road-worthiness tests for cars and light vans over a certain age in the 1960s, government officials did not themselves inspect millions of cars: road-worthiness certification was carried out by licensed private garages. At the time of writing, government is planning to adopt a similar system for heavy commercial vehicles, which had previously been subject to annual inspection by its own officials. Similarly, government is moving from a system whereby its health service doctors certificated unfitness to work to a regime of 'self-certification' by employees. This is exactly like moving from government-assessed to self-assessed taxation, as discussed in Chapter 4. One can argue seriously and at length about the possible side-effects of such instrument switching; but if it is 'bureaucracy' that government wants to save on, this is the direction in which it is likely to be led.

The same applies to passive as against active detection. We saw in Chapter 6 that active detection, almost by definition, requires more in the way of bureaucratic effort than passive detection; here again, a government bent on saving bureaucracy will tend to move from the former to the latter wherever they are substitutable. In Chapter 6 the example was given of a move from active to passive detection in the field of individual bankruptcy. Similarly, and for the same reason, government in Britain has switched from obligation-to-notify to obligation-to-display detectors in the case of trade names. From 1916 to 1982 all business trade names in Britain had to be registered with government, providing details of the individuals or companies behind those names. This enabled government to link trade names with the details of companies listed on its (separate) companies register. In 1982 government scrapped the register of business names and replaced it with obligation-to-display requirements for companies to disclose their true identity on their stationery and business premises (*The Times*, 22 March 1982).

Using 'contingently' rather than 'immanently' depletable resources

Saving on bureaucracy in a rather broader sense may point to using government resources that are 'contingently' rather than 'immanently' depletable. We have seen, from Chapter 1 onwards, how government can base its tool-kit on four basic resources, namely nodality, treasure, authority and organisation. Very roughly, it was suggested, these can be seen as involving an increasing scale of constraint.

There is another way of categorising these four basic resources which has only been touched upon so far and which is highly relevant to the idea of using government's resources sparingly. Two of them, treasure and organisation, are in most cases 'immanently depletable'. This means that these resources, by their nature, tend to be used *up* as they are used, unless they are replenished. Typically, the more of our treasure we use, the less we have left (exchanging one kind of treasure for another would not count as 'using' treasure in this sense). Similarly with organisation: it is the nature of government's armies, bureaucratic as well as military, that they have to be re-supplied; and, beyond some minimum point, the more they are used, the more they have to be re-supplied (if only to counter the effects of fatigue, hunger, wear and tear and enemy action). There may be isolated counter-examples (successful gambling might be one), but by and large we can suggest that treasure and organisation are immanently depletable, like fossil fuels.

Nodality and authority, however, are not like that. It is not in the nature of these resources that they are used up as they are used. Of course, they *may* be used up by applications which destroy government's credibility or legal standing; but, on the other hand, they may even be augmented as they are used. Using nodality successfully, for example, may actually increase government's nodality. The depletability of these resources is contingent, not immanent. In favourable circumstances they may not be depleting resources at all, but self-renewing or even self-augmenting ones: they are like wind and wave power, rather than fossil fuels.

If government wants to use its resources sparingly in a broader sense than merely limiting the number of 'bottoms on seats' on its payroll, this may point to using contingently rather than immanently depletable resources wherever those are substitutable. A fairly typical example of this was given in Chapter 5, showing how the British government in the early 1970s shifted the balance in anthrax prevention from direct action, in the form of elaborate factory operations, to tokens of authority relating to imported goods.

Minimising 'trouble, vexation and oppression' of government's subjects

If a government bent on 'using bureaucracy sparingly' in the first sense will tend to prefer general to particular instruments, passive to active instruments and instruments drawing on 'contingently' rather than 'immanently' depletable resources, what are the implications of using bureaucracy sparingly in the second sense? To follow the canon of not applying heavier bureaucratic tackle to the population at large than is strictly needed, it is suggested, will lead government to prefer low- to high-constraint instruments and what will be termed 'directional' instruments to non-directional ones.

Preferring low- to high-constraint instruments means preferring the use of nodality and treasure to the use of authority and organisation, wherever these are substitutable. Up to a point, this may take government in the same direction as 'using bureaucracy sparingly' in the first sense, as can be seen from Figure 8.1.

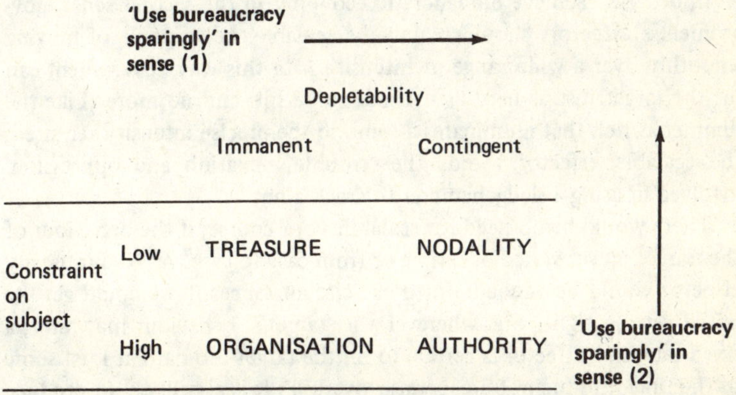

FIGURE 8.1 'Constraint' and 'depletability'

'Using bureaucracy sparingly' in both major senses would lead us to prefer nodality as a resource, because it involves low constraint *and* contingent depletability. Organisation, which has the reverse characteristics, would likewise be a resource to be avoided wherever possible for both reasons. It is mainly in the choice between treasure and authority that the two senses of 'using bureaucracy sparingly' would be likely to come into conflict, in terms of the different preferences they put on type of depletability as against level of constraint.

Preferring 'directional' to 'non-directional' instruments

If government aims to limit bureaucracy in the second sense, it will prefer 'directional' to 'non-directional' instruments, and this again is likely to lead to conflict with the implications of using bureaucracy sparingly in the first sense. 'Directional' tools are those which have the properties of 'scalability', 'directness' and 'non-substitutability', and these are likely to mean a preference for 'particular' tools that are bureaucracy-intensive in the first sense. Each of these 'directional' characteristics will be briefly discussed.

(1) *Scalability*. This term refers to the degree to which an instrument can be varied in its intensity. Most light switches have only two positions, 'on' and 'off'; but dimmer switches (as in theatres) enable the illumination of lamps to be increased or decreased by smooth increments. The latter are 'scalable'; the former are not.

In order to achieve bureaucratic economy in the second sense, government's effectors should plainly be scalable, i.e. capable of moving smoothly over a wide range of intensities. In this way government can hit the target just as hard as it needs to be hit, and no more. Like the dimmer switch that illuminates a room to the precise intensity required, the scalable effector avoids the 'trouble, vexation and oppression' involved in using a sledgehammer to crack a nut.

There would be no need for scalability, of course, if the behaviour of the 'target' never varied over time or from case to case. A fixed-intensity effector would be adequate in those circumstances if we could get the initial setting right. But wherever the 'target's' behaviour may vary, a fixed-intensity effector is certain to hit the target too hard at least some of the time, producing bureaucratic 'overkill'. It is also likely to produce 'underkill' at least some of the time; and indeed the more that government tries to avoid 'underkill' without scalability, for example by relying on the execution of offenders as the only penalty, the more serious is the overkill problem likely to be.

The problem is, of course, that it is difficult to build scalability into government effectors except by using 'particular' types that tend to be bureaucracy-intensive in the first sense. The same applies to 'directness'.

(2) *Directness*. In order to avoid visiting more 'bureaucracy' on the population at large than is absolutely necessary, government's instruments must not only be scalable; they must also be direct. 'Directness' refers to the precision with which an instrument can be directed to a specific beneficiary or maleficiary.

Here again, the problem is that government has to sacrifice directness whenever it uses a general instrument in order to influence the behaviour of an individual or a specific group. If the real target is struck at all – and it may not be – this is done only at the cost of hitting other targets that are not relevant. The effects cannot be confined to those against whom the action is really directed.

Examples of government effectors that do not hit the target 'cleanly' are not hard to find. Notoriously, blanket fines on business corporations for breaches of the law do not specifically reach the corporation officials who are directly responsible for those breaches (Stone, 1975, p. 50): at worst, they may just be an extra tax on the consumer. Bans on trade with a country whose government regime is disfavoured do not specifically reach those directly responsible for the character or behaviour of that regime: typically, those are the very last to suffer (Fisher, 1971). Threats of general tax increases to counter high pay demands will, if carried out, affect both those 'guilty' and those 'innocent' of such behaviour. Most of us are familiar with the phenomenon of group punishment from our schooldays, when a whole group is made to suffer for the acts of miscreants who cannot be identified or reached. One of the aspects of the eighteenth-century 'enlightenment' was the move by governments away from group punishments to the hanging, torture or mutilation of specific individuals (Stone, 1975), but the former have by no means entirely disappeared.

Indirect applications may sometimes be effective (they may actually reach the real target as well as hitting other targets). But the by-products or 'externalities' (in the language of economists) involved inevitably means involving non-combatants, as it were. It is not so much using a sledgehammer to crack a nut (the scalability problem) as of being obliged to use an instrument that is only capable of cracking pockets of nuts – not necessarily the ones we really want and more than we strictly require.

(3) *Substitutability or incidence.* A third feature of a 'directional' instrument is non-substitutability. Substitutability is closely related to directness. It refers to the extent to which an implement can be blunted or deflected from its target even if it is able to reach the target directly. To the extent that this can happen, there will again be a spillover of bureaucratic impact from the target to others.

Just as in reality taxes are commonly paid by people quite other than those who are legally responsible for paying the relevant money to the government, government's instruments in a wider sense often turn out to be shiftable even if they are direct. For example, government may be able to strike directly at an individual responsible for a motor offence by removing his (or her) driving licence. But the target individual may be able to deflect the blow in large part, even though in the sense of the last section it has fallen on him directly. He may, for instance, be able to take out insurance cover which provides for a chauffeur in the event of loss of licence. The insurance premiums may be underwritten by an employer and in effect 'paid' by the employer's customers in the prices they pay for services. In a case like this, substitutability renders the directness of the instrument nugatory.

The same may apply in many other circumstances. Companies may idemnify directors or other employees from government fines for the illegal actions they may perform (Stone, 1975; Cranston, 1979). Trade unions may be able to parry regulatory measures aimed at them by government, as did British trade unions in the early 1970s (Thomson and Engleman, 1975). Simply reaching the target, then, is not enough. Somehow the blow must be aimed so that it does not bounce or ricochet, if the impact is not to 'spill over' from the intended target.

Tools for the job: the problems of choice

By developing the implications of the 'economy' canon at somewhat greater length than the other three, some of the complexities of appraising government instruments can be seen. In this case, the problems go through at least four levels.

First, one cannot think of 'economising' without a basic understanding of the determinants of effectiveness, which is often absent in government administration. Even in building and engineering – activities, one might suppose, that are subject to relatively 'hard' laws of operation – there is a very fine line between maximum economy and ineffectiveness (perhaps disaster) through skimping on materials, meaning that a margin of error or tolerance has to be left. Materials are stronger and heavier than they absolutely need to be, according to theory.

When we come to administrative control, the same applies – only more so. Each context is unique: the content of the 'materials' used varies in several ways. The tolerances are in practice enormous. Often they are entirely unknown. Usually we do not know what might be the effect of using lighter or heavier bureaucratic tackle in this or that context; or, to change the metaphor, we can only guess the point at which the dam will break (Hood, 1976, p. 64). In practice, we often *do* end up building the administrative walls ten feet thick.

Second, 'economy' as a canon of choice plainly has to be balanced against other canons. Typically, for example, administrative cheapness has to be set against the unfairness or inconvenience that general or passive instruments may create.

Third, even if economy is preferred over other canons in cases of conflict, 'using bureaucracy sparingly' turns out to have at least two principal meanings which do not always drive in the same direction.

And fourth, even *within* each of those two principal meanings of 'economy' can be found sub-components which do not necessarily run together and which therefore have to be balanced one against the other. For example, not only is a preference for 'directional' instruments likely to conflict with a preference for 'general' ones: the components of 'directionality' may themselves have to be traded off against one another as government looks through the instruments which it might apply in any given case.

Balancing the components of 'directionality': a hypothetical example

Table 8.1 illustrates the last point with an imaginary, and exaggerated, case. It supposes that a government committed to the cause of vegetarianism has come to power. Fresh from its triumph, this government is considering which instruments in its tool-box may be deployed to promote the dictatorship of the vegetariat. Suppose further – somewhat unrealistically – that the possibilities were narrowed down to the eight set out in Table 8.1.

This is a contrived example, deliberately leaving out several options so that the eight shown conveniently cover the whole range of possible combinations of the three components of directionality. This means that all but one of them are less than fully directional, and that one – option (7), the custodial treatment of offenders – is, significantly, precisely the instrument that would be likely to encounter the heaviest political opposition. Short of employing that as a front-line measure, government would be forced to 'trade off' the advantages of one option against the advantages of another, or to use the options in 'matching opposite' combinations, such that the weakness of one instrument on some of the components of directionality was matched by pairing or combining it with another instrument with the opposite pattern of strength or weakness.

At first sight 'using bureaucracy sparingly' may appear an entirely

TABLE 8.1 Implementing a government drive for vegetarianism:

	(1)	(2)	(3)
Measure	Ban all meat imports	Fixed fines on firms for use of meat in food manufacture	Prohibit all meat-eating except at weekends
Parallel or analogy	Bans on import e.g. of pornographic material	Trading standards (fixed fines on firms for food adulteration, etc.)	Prohibition of alcohol, smoking, football
'Directionality'			
Scalability	No	No	No
Directness	No	No	Yes
Substitut-ability	No	Yes	No
Comment	Does not directly touch eaters of domestic meat	Miscreants may not be reached directly; costs can be passed on in prices	Blunt instrument; can't be turned up or down

common-sense and unexceptionable idea. Press the idea a little further, however, and it turns out to present difficult choices at several levels.

Conclusion

The four possible canons for 'good application' of government's instruments that have been discussed in this chapter indicate some of the practical difficulties involved in judging those instruments as good or

eight possible measures

(4) Government propaganda for vegetarianism	(5) Limit sales of meat to registered addicts	(6) Threaten to raise general taxes if aggregate meat consumption does not fall	(7) Treat individual meat-eaters (by aversion therapy, etc.)	(8) Meat rationing through a coupon scheme
Health education (e.g. against smoking, drinking, glue-sniffing)	Control of drug sales, etc.	Tax amnesties, 'open compacts' in wage controls	Treatment of alcoholics, etc.	General rationing (in wartime, etc.)
Yes	No	Yes	Yes	Yes
No	Yes	No	Yes	Yes
No	Yes	Yes	No	Yes
Message goes to vegetarians as well as to meat-eaters	Registered addicts could re-sell supplies	Falls on 'guilty' and 'innocent' alike; tax costs could be passed on	Fully 'directional'	Rations could be exchanged

bad, except on a highly pragmatic and individualistic trial-and-error basis. Each of the canons discussed here quickly becomes faltering and ambiguous when it is examined carefully.

Moreover, as applies to Adam Smith's principles of taxation, the canons may conflict with one another at the margin. For example, effectiveness and economy might point to the use of government instruments that would attract moral censure as unduly coercive. This was the case in our imaginary example of a government drive for vegetarianism. As we will see in Chapter 9, some see this conflict as lying at the heart of the 'government effectiveness problem' in modern democracies. Indeed, if you spin the wheel again, you can find conflicting canons *within* each canon, as we have just seen with 'economy'.

It is perhaps futile to look for purely intellectual ways of 'resolving' such conflicts. The political process does that. Governments in different circumstances will give primacy to different canons; and indeed the relative emphasis given to each canon is likely to alter continuously with every shift of the political wind. For example, a long period of evident failure in some endeavour is likely to put the emphasis on the first and second canons, accentuating and extending government's search for alternative tools for the job. On the other hand, the advent of a highly 'ideological' regime after a political upheaval may give more importance to the third canon, requiring each act to be justified in terms of the high-flown principles to which the new regime adheres. Again, a government in 'fiscal crisis' – a problem which overtook many Western governments in the 1970s – may well give more emphasis to the final canon of economy, taking an urgent interest in ways of making government cheaper. But when it is government's very existence, rather than its 'store of treasure', that is in question, effectiveness is likely to elbow out the other canons: defeat the enemy, by fair means or foul, and damn the expense.

9 A Changing Mix of Government Tools?

> **By now we should have learned to ask not only what government can promise but what in fact it can do.**
>
> (Wildavsky, 1980, p. 45)

In this brief final chapter we switch from thinking about how to appraise government's use of its instruments to looking at those instruments in a wider perspective. The chapter is divided into two main sections. The first section explores ways in which the overall mix of government's instruments can change. Looking mainly at writing about developed Western countries and at pieces of British evidence, it considers whether there has been any discernable direction of change in the broad mix of government tools in the recent past. One of the themes of earlier chapters was the way government can ring the changes, using different instruments to address this or that subject over time. But we have not so far considered changes in the tools used by government as a whole.

The second section, which concludes both the chapter and the book, briefly considers some of the *limitations* of government's instruments. Up till now we have tended to stress the possibilities of government's tool-box, not its limitations. But the possibilities are not, of course, limitless. Government's tools are not like the magic rings, lamps or charms we read about in fairy tales. Indeed, there are many circumstances in which 'overload' or misuse can prevent those instruments from operating as government might wish. One of those circumstances is 'overload' in the sense of declining acceptability of government among its subjects at large, which was a thread running through many of the earlier chapters.

Change over time: the mixture as before?

Up to now I have tried to show that government in practice always involves some mixture of the whole gamut of tools discussed in this book. There may be single-tool agencies, but there is no such thing as single-tool government. However, as was shown for each of the classes of tools discussed in Parts I and II, the overall mixture can change over time, with different elements becoming dominant.

Exactly the same point can be made for government as a whole. Government might put the emphasis on propaganda to shape the knowledge and attitudes of its subjects, for example. It might put the emphasis on official tokens, to create a style of regulatory government. It might stress government by cheque-book or by direct action. Or it might put the emphasis on surveillance, concentrating on the acquisition of information about its subjects. And the balance may shift among these emphases from time to time, or even all the time.

In practice, of course, gauging what shifts in emphasis have in fact taken place can be difficult or impossible. Take the common argument, touched upon in Chapter 6, that government nowadays is putting more emphasis on detection, shifting towards a 'surveillance state' – a government that is all eyes and ears, as it were. Everyone is now familiar with the argument that developments in electronics, as well as possibly returning government bureaucracy to its nineteenth-century scale of small business or even of 'cottage industry', can dramatically expand government's detection capacity by increasing the ability to store, collate and cross-reference information. Writers on the 'data bank society' (for example Madgwick and Smythe, 1974) see an increased tendency for government to gather general intelligence about its subjects in a pre-emptive way, browsing through their affairs and applying a military practice to society at large.

Forceful examples have been adduced to such writers to support the proposition of a move in the direction of a 'surveillance state'. Such a shift in emphasis, if that is really what is taking place, could have important implications. But it cannot actually be demonstrated one way or the other, since there is no aggregate index that registers change in the use of government's detectors.

Perhaps the proposition is so self-evident that it needs no demonstration? Sceptics might not think so. The ability to store, collate and retrieve data (which is the main thrust of the 'information revolution') is not the same thing as the ability to collect information from society in the first place. Only the latter is 'detection' in the sense used in this book. And detection capacity in that sense might in fact be reduced if, as is quite plausible, knowledge of government's increased information-processing ability raises social resistance to government's attempts to gather information (see Campbell in Hain, 1980, p. 139). Indeed, even where the technology does relate directly to detection, new developments may just 'raise the ante' where government and its subjects are in conflict, as was mentioned in Chapter 6. Such developments may in reality do no more than enable government to keep abreast of new types of communication rather than tipping the scales of surveillance decisively in government's favour as compared with the past.

From regulatory government to cheque-book government – and back?

The same problem applies to the question of whether government in recent times has put more or less emphasis on regulation by official tokens. Such a mode of government is hard to pin down in numbers. The 'currency' is elusive to measurement. Rose (1981, p. 22) cites indicators that suggest that the annual number of orders under delegated legislation (Statutory Instruments) in Britain has not changed markedly since the 1940s, and that the number of Acts of Parliament passed annually has actually declined since the early years of this century. Something similar seems to have happened in the USA. But, as Rose concedes, merely counting laws passed and orders declared is at best a crude representation: ideally, we should weigh as well as count, since not all official tokens are of equal importance. Moreover, as we saw in Chapter 4, many of government's official tokens (such as certificates, licences, permits) are not cast in the form of laws or statutory instruments, and would not be picked up if we only counted these high-level types.

It is therefore not clear whether the overall incidence of regulatory government has increased or decreased, at least as far as the United Kingdom and the USA are concerned. But conventional wisdom certainly has it that the hallmark of nineteenth-century government was 'regulatory' activity, i.e. reliance on official tokens rather than on achieving government's aims through mass propaganda or a barrage of money payments. In the twentieth century government in the United Kingdom began to place more emphasis on direct action, starting up and operating such things as wool disinfection factories, breweries and public houses. As has been shown elsewhere (Hood and Dunsire, 1981, pp. 11 and 247), the growth of the British central bureaucracy in the first half of the twentieth century outstripped the growth of public spending in constant-price terms as government came to undertake more activities itself.

Since the 1950s the emphasis has changed again, this time with a shift towards an era of 'cheque-book government' at central level. This has happened both in the United Kingdom and in the USA. The central civil service of both countries has remained almost constant in size since that time (Heclo, in King, 1978; Hood and Dunsire, 1981, p. 11, Table 1.1), while government spending has increased two- or threefold in real terms.

Table 9.1 shows what has happened to government's overall spending profile in Britain over a twenty-year period from the early 1960s to the early 1980s. If we take the cost of employing government's central officials, judges and military forces as a crude index of government's do-it-yourself activities, it can be seen that this item has fallen noticeably over the period as a proportion of government's budget. Subsidies have risen and fallen in a dramatic way, while grants by central government to the world outside have risen noticeably as a proportion of government's budget.

TABLE 9.1 Is government moving towards an increasingly money-moving style?

	Percentage of government budget*		
	1961–2	1971–2	1981–2
Cost of government's armed forces, civil service and judiciary	31.4	25.1	23.5
Government subsidies (for food, agricultural produce, etc.)	11.1	39.1	5.5
Grants from central government	29.5	38.8	40.7
Of which: Grants to persons	8.4	8.5	16.9

* = estimated expenditure to be voted by Parliament, excluding money earned by government in fees, etc.

Sources: Chief Secretary of the Treasury's Memorandum on the Supply Estimates, HC 142 Session 1961–2, Cmnd 4627, 1971, and Cmnd 8184, 1981.

This is fragmentary evidence, drawn from only one country, and highly aggregated. Indeed, some individual government departments in Britain have moved towards a rather *less* money-moving style over this period, for example the Home Office, the Department of Trade and the Scottish Office. But it is the aggregate picture that interests us here, and that picture is clearly one of an increased emphasis on the cheque-book.

Many authors have noticed the tendency for government, at least in countries like the United Kingdom and the USA, to have placed increased emphasis on the money-moving tool in the recent past, and correspondingly less emphasis on direct action or on regulation by means of official tokens. Such a change however, can, be interpreted in more than one way. Writers such as Bardach (1977) and Wildavsky (1980) interpret it as a move towards the kind of tasks that government can carry out with some modicum of effectiveness, and away from tasks that government finds impossible to carry out in practice. As Wildavsky (1980, p. 2) observes:

> It helps to learn what government is worse at doing (changing citizens' behaviour) and what it is better at doing (moving money). Then we would be less surprised that citizens are better able to get government to change what it does than they are at getting government to change the way that their fellow-citizens behave.

The change towards an increased emphasis on cheque-book government can be interpreted in different, if not necessarily contradictory, ways. For example, Marxists such as Fainstein and Fainstein (in Weiss and Barton, 1980, p. 20) believe that the development of modern capitalism has a tendency to strip from government the control over 'the means of public administration'. This is a neat parallel with the well known Marxist argument that workers under a capitalist system cease to control the means of production, as ownership comes to be concentrated in other hands. In this case the argument goes that there are structural biases in the political system which tend to force government to approach society by means of 'arm's length' instruments rather than to go into business for itself, especially when it comes to those activities which, if undertaken in private business, can produce a profit.

Such observations can of course lead to exactly the same conclusions as those drawn by Wildavsky and Bardach, in that a government facing such 'structural biases' is cut off from precisely those tools that *would* be most likely to have a powerful effect on its subjects' behaviour, especially when it comes to policies involving fundamental behaviour modification among the public at large. It is a question of whether those structural biases are to be linked with pressures exerted specifically by capitalism or from the preferences embedded in democratic or neo-liberal politics (Simon, Smithburg and Thompson, 1950, p. 21; Scharpf, 1979, pp. 20–2). Indeed, the change could even be interpreted in a way diametrically opposite to the Marxist interpretation, by assuming that modern government has so effectively 'colonised' the world outside that the latter will be more responsive to government's stimuli than in the past, rendering a resort to official tokens and direct action less necessary.

Moreover, whatever may be the correct interpretation of the change towards cheque-book government at central level in recent decades in some countries, it is quite possible that this change is being highlighted by social analysts just as the emphasis is starting to shift once again. This is a common fate of such observations. At the end of Chapter 8 it was pointed out that a government in 'fiscal crisis' may put heavy emphasis on the 'economy' canon, looking urgently for cheaper tools to perform any given job. And, of course, the 'fiscal crisis of the state' (O'Connor, 1973; Rose and Peters, 1978; Hood and Wright, 1981) is in reality a well known and widespread phenomenon, which has the effect of threatening government's capacity precisely at the cheque-book or hip-pocket level.

Under such circumstances it is quite possible that government might come once more to put increasing emphasis on tokens of authority rather than on its cheque-book (Scharpf, 1979, p. 24). In previous chapters several examples have been given of the substitution of official tokens for direct action as a means of cutting down government's costs. The scope for direct substitution may not be so great in the case of money-moving and official tokens, but nevertheless government might shift the balance of emphasis at the margin. Such a change in emphasis would not, of course, make government 'smaller' in anything but an accountant's sense (loose talk of 'privatisation' in such circumstances can be misleading). But that is precisely the advantage for a government in fiscal crisis: 'creeping government' in the form of tokens of authority is hard to track down in aggregate, and it has the further great advantage of throwing 'compliance costs' on to government's subjects rather than itself.

Government by propaganda?

Another possible way in which the balance of emphasis might shift is in the direction of increased stress on information-dispensing and propaganda. J. K. Galbraith (1971, p. 208) develops the argument that modern propaganda and advertising techniques have greatly increased the ability of organisations to persuade a mass public, especially in circumstances where 'primary needs' (such as basic shelter and sustenance) have been met. Such techniques, Galbraith thinks, erode the need for cruder tools for influencing social behaviour.

If this is right, it might suggest that governments, especially in 'affluent' countries, might be putting more stress on persuasion and propaganda than in the past. Galbraith is certainly not alone in stressing the importance of persuasion as an instrument. Lasswell, Lerner and Speier (1980, Vol. III, p. 531) write of the increasing political importance of propaganda. Lyman and Scott (1975) talk of 'theatrocracy', or rule by theatrical show, as was mentioned in Chapter 2. Edelman (1971, 1977) repeatedly stresses the importance of government's symbolic activities and their being frequently more powerful than its more 'contrete' activities. This is a classical theme.

But is government putting more weight on propagandising instruments now than in the past? This is, of course, another of those impossible questions. One way of looking for a clue is to find out what government spends on information output. Table 9.2 gives a few key elements in central government's budget in Britain in the early 1950s and in the early 1980s. The bottom line of the table shows the share of government spending on information at home and overseas through the medium of its official propaganda office, the Central Office of Information.

At first sight there does not seem to be much support here for the idea of modern government as increasingly relying on propaganda weapons. As can be seen, the picture is one of relative stagnation in propaganda as a proportion of the total. In fact it has fallen slightly over the period. The proportion of the British central government's budget devoted to propaganda in the early 1950s was double the proportion spent on prisons. By the early 1980s it was the other way round. Perhaps Britain is untypical; but this does not quite square with the idea of government as turning away from duress to propaganda.

Nevertheless, this is a somewhat ambiguous indicator. It is a measure of input, not a measure of output. It might be argued that increasing

TABLE 9.2 Duress or propaganda? Percentage of British central government spending on four selected items, 1950–1 and 1980–1*

	1950–1	1980–1
Police (mainland Britain)	0.9	1.5
Prisons (mainland Britain)	0.2	0.6
Armed forces	23.2	22.5
Home and overseas information	0.5	0.3

* = estimated expenditure to be voted by Parliament, excluding money earned by government in fees, etc.

Sources: Civil Estimates for 1950–1, HC 2–7, Session 1950; Government Information Services Cmd 8267 1951; Supply Estimates for 1980–1 HC 470 – ix Session 1979–80 (Class IX – Law, Order and Protective Services); and *Memorandum by the Chief Secretary of the Treasury on the Supply Estimates* 1980–1, Cmnd 7869, 1980.

ability to manipulate social behaviour through advertising techniques could cause the 'productivity' of such spending to rise. If so, this would mean that the 1980–1 'propaganda pound' bought far more behavioural modification than did the 1950–1 propaganda pound – and hence that a constant or even slightly falling budget for this item, in terms of its share of total government spending, conceals a growth in its social significance as a weapon of government.

Alternatively (or additionally) it could be that government since the 1950s has so effectively 'colonised' the free media, that is, press, radio and TV, that it no longer needs to spend huge sums in order to influence the population at large. The expensive mass-propaganda techniques that were so popular with Western governments in the 1940s – travelling government exhibitions, government poster campaigns, government-made films – became clumsy and redundant. All that government now needs to do is to 'manage the news', by stage-managing pseudo-events that will capture the attention of the free media and, through them, the public at large (a good discussion, in relation to the modern US presidency, is found in Hodgson, 1980, chapter 6). Such methods are now a commonplace for publicists and promoters of all kinds. This, too, might mean that the falling share of propaganda spending in government's budget was consistent with an expansion of the power of government information-dispensers, not a decline.

Here again, even taking only one country, the direction of change is hard to establish. There is no convenient metric such as applies to government spending. And even if it were indeed true that government nowadays places more emphasis on propaganda than it did in the past, this would still be open to more than one interpretation. It could be seen as demonstrating the increased power of information-dispensing as an effector, as Galbraith seems to believe but many deny (such as Friedman, 1977, and Hodgson, 1980). Or it could, on the contrary, be seen in the same way as some read the shift to 'cheque-book government', i.e. as reflecting the limits imposed on modern government by the pressures of democracy and/or capitalism. It would be another manifestation of government's being steered towards the choice of its least effective behaviour-changing instruments rather than its most effective ones.

Government by duress?

Other kinds of change in the overall balance of emphasis among government's instruments are possible. Those who see government as facing rising discontent will doubt the magic of its hip pocket or of its propaganda. For example, Marxists who believe in a crisis of capitalism and a growing challenge to modern government arising from popular dissatisfaction and increased trade union militancy, might expect to see a different kind of shift in the use of government's tool-kit. They might expect government under those circumstances to have to resort to increasingly coercive instruments in order to retain its precarious authority. Police, prisons and the armed forces of government would become front-line instruments in the class struggle. This would be a shift to 'government by duress' – a style of government whose chief concern is to coerce its enemies into submission.

This is, of course, a familiar picture in many parts of the world. Indeed, few governments can avoid switching to a 'coercive' style on occasion. For example, Lowi and Stone (1978, pp. 26–7) point to some evidence of increasing use of federal troops in civil policing operations in the USA from the mid-1960s. As far as Britain is concerned, if we look back to Table 9.2, we might detect some slight indication of a shift towards government by duress. Government's spending on police and prisons in mainland Britain did increase markedly as a proportion of central government's total budget between 1950–1 and 1980–1. Expenditure on police grew by more than 50 per cent as a proportion of government's budget, and the share of expenditure on prisons more than doubled, increasing by over three times the percentage increase in total central government current expenditure from 1950 to the mid-1970s.

Nor was the rise in the share of government's spending allotted to prisons just a matter of it costing more to do the same job, a phenomenon familiar in government as the 'relative price effect' (Rose, 1981, p. 21). There is no doubt that British government makes greater resort to imprisonment now than it did in the early 1950s (Cmnd 7673, 1979; Cmnd 7749, 1979). The prison population has more than doubled over that period, from below 20,000 people to nearly 50,000, and this in spite of continual attempts to reduce that population by such means as suspended sentences and greater use of parole. The increase has, of course, been more dramatic in Northern Ireland, where the prison population trebled during the eight years from 1970 to 1978, but that would not affect the 'mainland' figures given in Table 9.2.

The significance of these changes, however, should not be exaggerated. Even for a relatively 'gaol-happy' government like the British, maintaining its prisons still amounts to less than a penny in every pound that government spends. Indeed, even if the cumulative growth rates of prison spending in relation to government's total spending were to be the same over the twenty-five years subsequent to 1975 as they were in the previous twenty-five years, prison spending would still be slightly less than 3 per cent of British central government spending by the year 2000. Moreover, as can be seen from Table 9.2, the proportion of government's budget that was spent on the armed forces was not markedly different in 1980–1 from what it was in 1950–1. Indeed, the combined share of all three major components of government's apparatus for duress – police, prisons and armed forces – was almost exactly the same in 1980–1 (24.6 per cent) as it had been thirty years earlier (24.3 per cent). Altogether this hardly amounts to a clear picture of a major shift towards government by duress.

Even for a single country – which may well be untypical – there is clearly no hard and fast way of discovering what has happened to the relative weight placed on some of government's major instruments over the past thirty years. For some of them, we lack even rudimentary clues, in spite of a great deal of debate and argument about government 'growth' and allegedly increased 'intervention' in social affairs. The one thing that does seem fairly clear is that government, at least in the USA and Britain, has placed increasing reliance on its cheque-book in the recent past. But is this an emphasis that can be sustained, let alone increased, at a time of faltering economic growth and of rising 'fiscal stress'? Questions of 'overload' are raised in such circumstances; and it is to that issue that we turn in the concluding section. Can government's tool-box be 'overloaded', and if so, how?

Overloading government's tool-kit?

'Overload' is a common theme in discussions of the problems of modern government, especially, but not exclusively, in the liberal-democratic West. The term is often used in a vague sense. Broadly it is used to denote what is seen as a chronic tendency for governments to become weighed down by demands which they lack the capacity to satisfy, financially and administratively overstretched, facing an increasingly hostile or indifferent environment. Government, so it is said, is constantly being pressed to step into new fields, take over and 'solve' new problems, perhaps partly becoming a victim of its own apparent success with other problems in the past (Brittan, 1975: King, 1975; Rose and Peters, 1978; Wildavsky, 1980). When pressures and expectations outrun government's capacity to deliver, a gap opens up between demands or aspirations and government performance, i.e. what it can actually do with the tools and resources available to it.

When the tools will not serve

Up till now, as was mentioned earlier, the book has stressed the possibilities rather than the limitations of government's tool-kit: it has looked at the many possible applications to which a quite limited set of basic instruments can be put, and the complex patterns into which they can be arranged. But there is, of course, another side to the coin. Government's tools, however skilfully they are used, do not enable it to shape the world outside in any way that it likes. There are some inherent limitations. Others depend on circumstances.

The inherent limitations are obvious enough. There are some problems which government instruments cannot even in principle effectively engage. No government tool can solve problems of this kind directly; any attempt to do so would be better termed mis-application rather than overload. For example, government ultimately cannot protect people from their own foolish hopes, such as those of making easy money on an ever-rising stock market. Of course, there are many things that government can do to address such 'problems' indirectly. It might ban private stock markets altogether. It might use official tokens to control stock exchange fees, practices and operators, as did the US government when it created the Securities and Exchange Commission after the great stock market crash of 1929 (Kohlmeier, 1969). But that is *all* government can do; and neither of these approaches solves the problem directly. The first kills the patient as well as the disease. The second tackles the symptoms rather than the illness itself.

There are many other situations in which the same thing applies. No government instrument can convey to its subjects a right to happiness, although government may be able to give rights or means for the *pursuit* of happiness (Sennett, 1977, p. 90; Baechler, 1979). No government can satisfy incompatible demands, although it may be able to offer conciliation, impose arbitration, give the rhetoric to one side and the decision to the other (Edelman, 1971, p. 39). To the extent that government is pressed or expected to deal with such 'problems' directly, none of its tools will do the job.

In other cases, government's tools are not necessarily limited in their inherent capacity to tackle a problem, but circumstances may undermine that capacity. This can come about in several ways: the 'production function' for the task in hand may be unknown; or government may use its instruments in a deliberately ham-fisted way; or the field of application may be too recalcitrant for some of those instruments to work effectively. A brief comment will be made on each of these circumstances.

First, government's tools will not do the job if it is pressed to deal with problems to which those tools might in principle be applied, but for which no effective production function is in fact known. There may be no well worked-out technology at hand. Cause-and-effect relationships may be poorly understood, requiring blind faith or guesswork in foreseeing how this or that instrument may affect the issue.

This harks back to the second canon for tool selection ('matching the tool to the job') in Chapter 8; and as everybody knows, government very often *does* find itself addressing tasks for which the production function is poorly understood. This is a commonplace of writing on public policy: the prevention of crime, the quelling of riots and the generation of better economic performance are only some of the more obvious cases in point. We cannot say *a priori* that the job is impossible, but no one actually seems to know how to do it. The same may sometimes apply to more narrowly technical projects that government may want to undertake, although problems with machine technology (rather than 'social technology' in a broader sense) are probably not typical (King, 1975).

Second, government's tools may fail to perform a job even if the production function is clear, because of the way in which government chooses, or is pressed, to apply them. For example, fiscal stress may lead government to apply itself to a certain task with lighter bureaucratic tackle than is really needed, avoiding financial give-aways or bureaucracy-intensive methods when that is what is required to do the job properly. Similarly, political stress might press government to employ over-light tackle in a different sense, for instance in attempting to modify social behaviour in a fundamental way by the use of low-constraint instruments that are bound to be less than fully effective. This is a situation commonly diagnosed by commentators on public policy, as we saw in the last section.

Nor is it only a matter of the weight of tackle employed, in the various senses that 'weight' can have. The same sort of problem can arise when government puts its tools to work in contradictory ways, so that the effects cancel one another out, or at least are drastically damped by tools being used for contradictory purposes. One government agency may put out information to counteract the information being put out by other government agencies – something which is commonly observable in the case of rival regional development agencies. Or one agency's deeds may work against another agency's words. For example, the French government on the one hand manufactures and sells tobacco (through its traditional fiscal monopoly) and on the other hand warns the public of the dangers of smoking.

Such things are all too likely to happen when government pursues its activities through a dense and overlapping multi-bureaucratic structure, the pieces of which are frequently at cross-purposes with one another (King, 1975; Hogwood, 1979; Wildavsky, 1980). In such circumstances – commonplace in many modern states – government's tools may 'fail it', even if the job is feasible and the production function perfectly well known.

This, too, is more a case of 'misapplication' – wilful or otherwise – of government's tools rather than 'overload' in any engineering sense. But in many cases 'failures' of government tools are precisely of this kind. For example, business regulation failures – when avoidable accidents occur or regulated companies go bankrupt in a damaging way – often involve misapplications of perfectly well known administrative tools. Problems of this kind far more commonly result from the failure to use existing tools properly (especially detectors and official tokens) than from the inherent difficulty of adapting government tools to new machine technologies.

Finally, government's tools may falter, however determined or single-minded government may be, because conflict between government and its subjects will make some tools inapplicable or ineffective and others perhaps counter-productive. Declining consensus and rising disaffection may force government to change its overall mix of tools, often in ways which may serve to aggravate rather than to damp down those pressures and which may result in a decline in government's absolute performance. This was a theme running through Parts I and II in the discussion of the effects that increased pressure on government might have on each major class of tools.

What that discussion implied was that some government effectors are essentially 'fair-weather' instruments. For instance, 'prompted query responses', 'packaged self-serve' and 'privished' messages all require an interested public that is 'cued in' to the information which government chooses to hand out. Similarly, certificates rely for their effect on general respect for government, so that its stamp of approval is valued by society at large. Conditional tokens rely on the belief that government can be trusted to keep its word. Cheque-book government, it was suggested, presupposes a society in which government is regarded at least in a fairly neutral way by the bulk of its subjects.

When the weather turns foul, i.e. the mood of the crowd turns ugly and government faces rising social hostility or distrust, tools such as these have to be downgraded or put away. If demand-triggered information-dispensers cannot be used, government has to turn to direct notification propaganda, stuffing its message down its subjects' throats and putting more emphasis on fielding uninvited demands for information as it tries to prevent its secrets from coming into the limelight.

Similarly, as we saw in Chapter 4, government in such circumstances may have to move the emphasis away from certification. Even enablements and conditional tokens may cease to answer at some point, forcing government to put more stress on constraints and thus putting its authority 'on the line' in the most direct way. The cheque-book mode of government may come under pressure, as people become less likely to be swayed from one course of action to another by financial incentives, more distrustful of accepting government's money, especially when to do so is to be tainted in the eyes of powerful forces that are hostile to the government. This means that the overall balance may have to shift in the direction of government tools for direct action, based on the resource of organisation.

All of these changes, of course, make government more exposed and more intrusive. Most of them, as we have seen, serve to make it much more expensive as well. Such shifts may thus serve to worsen the social climate that prompted them in the first place.

Much the same can happen with detecting tools, as we saw in Chapter 6. Rising social hostility to government is likely to cause a relative shift from passive to active modes of scrutiny, and from nodal receivers and rewards to requisitions and ergonomic detectors, once again involving a move from the 'low-constraint' resources of nodality and treasure to the higher-constraint resources of authority and organisation. Government may have to step up its own 'snooping' efforts, if its subjects become less inclined to 'shop' their fellows to its officials. It may have to increase the intensity and lower the degree of selection of its investigations in order to obtain the same amount of information that it could get in more consensual times.

Here again, government is obliged to adjust its mix of detection tools in a way that will tend to increase the intrusiveness of its activities and likewise will tend to increase the scope and cost of its bureaucracy by an enormous amount. And that, too, may serve to aggravate rather than damp down the decline in its social acceptability.

Conclusion

When government's tool-kit becomes 'overloaded' in a general sense, it finds itself trapped in a series of vicious 'positive feedback' loops of this kind. The syndrome is all too recognisable in many places. But if the rough and ready indicators discussed in the last section are any guide, there is little indication that government in Britain is moving in these kinds of directions. Signs of 'overload' of this kind may certainly be discernable in places such as big-city slum ghettoes and troubled areas like Ulster. But there appears to be little overall sign over thirty years of an increase in government propaganda efforts, not much indication of increasing duress, and still less of a shift from cheque-book government to direct action. In some ways, one might almost speak of lessening load.

So far as the developed countries are concerned, probably the same would apply in most cases. For these, mis-application of government's tool-kit seems more likely to arise than overload in a narrower, engineering-type sense. Indeed, precisely for this reason, governments in the future – and citizens making demands on those governments – may need to become more aware of what is in government's tool-box in order to develop a better understanding of the possibilities and limitations of what government can do. Growing fiscal pressure, continuing high ambitions or expectations of government, and an increasing density of government and international activities will all tend to cause governments to search more diligently round their tool-shed for new combinations of instruments or tools that can be carried over from one context to another. Traditional, taken-for-granted assumptions about what instruments can be applied to which contexts may increasingly need to be re-examined.

Briefly, and in plain language, success in government, in the future as in the past, will depend on its ability to apply a relatively fixed set of basic tools imaginatively to each new situation as it arises.

Guide to Further Reading

The 'tool-kit' approach to government that is taken in this book is unorthodox, and many diffuse sources have been drawn upon. The discussion, especially in Parts I and II, leads off into many specialist subjects for which it would be impossible to sketch out a reading guide here.

There is space here only to refer to a few sources relevant to the central idea of the book, namely that of looking at government activities as the application of a set of tools or instruments. The reader who wishes to follow up this idea might perhaps begin by exploring three main traditions of thought.

One is the age-old discussion of political power and authority. Two 'old classics' with useful inventories of basic sources of power and authority are Simon, Smithburg and Thompson (1950, especially ch. 8, pp. 180–201) and Lasswell and Kaplan (1950, especially ch. 5, pp. 74–102). Wrong (1979, pp. 24 and 65) offers a fairly up-to-date commentary on 'power' and classifies types of power in a fairly traditional way.

Second is the variety of classification of modes of government action resulting from the growth of 'public policy' studies since the 1960s. Some of these are fairly similar to the approach taken here. A few useful sources are Lowi (1964, pp. 677–715), Froman and Salisbury (both in Ranney, 1968, respectively pp. 41–52 and 151–75), Offe (1975, especially ch. 3, pp. 82–100), Rose (1976), Mayntz (1977 and 1980, especially pp. 1–17), Kaufmann (in Grunow and Hegner, 1980, pp. 29–43) and Hogwood (1981). For those who read German, a good review of a wide range of classifications is to be found in Kaufmann and Rosewitz (1982).

Third is the tradition of cybernetics and systems theory. There are many good basic introductions applying these ideas to social and government matters. Useful starting points are Kramer and de Smit (1977), Ashby (1956), Beer (1972), Klaus (1973) and Dunsire (1978).

References

1. British parliamentary publications

Bankruptcy: A Consultative Document, Cmnd 7967 (HMSO, 1980).
Interception of Communications: Report of the Committee of Privy Councillors, Cmnd 283 (HMSO, 1957).
Prisons in Scotland: Report for 1978, Cmnd 7749 (HMSO, 1979).
Report of the Committee of Inquiry into the UK Prison Services, Cmnd 7673 (HMSO, 1979).
Security of the Census of Population, Cmnd 5365 (HMSO, 1973).

2. Other sources

Alderman, G., 'Jews and Sunday Trading: The Use and Abuse of Delegated Legislation', *Public Administration*, 60 (1982) pp. 99–104.
Arendt, H., *Between Past and Future* (Viking Press, 1961).
Ashby, W. R., *An Introduction to Cybernetics* (Barnes & Noble, 1956).
Baechler, J., *Suicides* (Blackwell, 1979).
Bardach, E., *The Implementation Game: What Happens After A Bill Becomes a Law* (MIT Press, 1977).
Barnes, D. and Reid, E., *Government and Trade Unions: The British Experience 1964–79* (Heinemann, 1980).
Beer, S., *Brain of the Firm* (Allen Lane, 1972).
Binney, J. E. D., *British Public Finance and Administration 1774–92* (Oxford University Press, 1958).
Bradshaw, J., *The Family Fund: An Initiative in Social Policy* (Routledge & Kegan Paul, 1980).
Breyer, S. G., *Regulation and Its Reform* (Harvard University Press, 1982).
Brittan, S., 'Economic Contradictions of Democracy', *British Journal of Political Science*, V (1975) pp. 129–59.
Brown, J. A. C., *Techniques of Persuasion: From Propaganda to Brainwashing* (Penguin, 1963).
Campbell, D., 'Society under Surveillance', in Hain, P. *et al.* (eds) *Policing the Police*, Vol. II (Calder, 1980).

Chapman, L., *Your Disobedient Servant* (Chatto & Windus, 1978).

Clark, Sir F., *Central Office of Information* (Allen & Unwin, 1971).

Colby, W. and Forbath, P., *Honorable Men: My Life in the CIA* (Simon & Schuster, 1978).

Congressional Quarterly Weekly Report, XXXIX, 40 (3 Oct 1981) p. 1899.

Conquest, R., *Kolyma: The Arctic Death Camps* (Macmillan, 1978).

Cornford, J., 'The Prospects for Privacy', *Political Quarterly* LII, 3 (July–September 1981) pp. 295–313.

Cranston, R., *Regulating Business* (Macmillan, 1979).

Crombie, Sir J., *HM Customs and Excise* (Allen & Unwin, 1962).

Dromey, J. and Taylor, G., *Grunwick: The Workers' Story* (Lawrence & Wishart, 1978).

Dunne, F. P., *Mr Dooley in Peace and War* (Richards, 1899).

Dunsire, A., *The Execution Process*, 2 vols (Robertson, 1978).

Edelman, M., *Politics as Symbolic Action: Mass Arousal and Quiescence* (Markham, 1971).

Edelman, M., *Political Language: Words That Succeed and Policies That Fail* (Academic Press, 1977).

Enzensberger, H. M., 'Constituents of a Theory of the Media', *New Left Review*, 64 (November–December 1970) pp. 13–36.

Etzioni-Halevy, E., *Political Manipulation and Administrative Power: A Comparative Study* (Routledge & Kegan Paul, 1979).

Fagen, R. R., *Politics and Communication: An Analysis* (Little, Brown, 1966).

Fainstein, S. S. and Fainstein, N. I., 'The Political Economy of American Bureaucracy', in Weiss, C. H. and Barton, A. H. (eds), *Making Bureaucracies Work* (Sage, 1980) pp. 279–97.

Fisher, R., *Basic Negotiating Strategy: International Conflict for Beginners* (Allen Lane, 1971).

Friedman, M., 'From Galbraith to Economic Freedom', Occasional Paper 49 (Institute of Economic Affairs, 1977).

Froman, L. A., Jr., 'The Categorization of Policy Contents', in Ranney, A. (ed.) *Political Science and Public Policy* (Markham, 1968) pp. 41–52.

Fry, G. K., *The Growth of Government* (Cass, 1979).

Galbraith, J. K., *The New Industrial State*, 2nd edn (Houghton Mifflin, 1971).

Gatti, J. F., *The Limits of Government Regulation* (Academic Press, 1981).

Giddings, P. J., *Marketing Boards and Ministers* (Saxon House, 1974).

Grunow, D. and Hegner, F. (eds) *Welfare or Bureaucracy? Problems of Matching Social Services to Clients' Needs* (Oelgeschlager, Gunn & Hain, 1980).

Gunsteren, H. R. van, 'The Ethical Context of Bureaucracy and Performance Analysis' (ZiF, Universität Bielefeld, 1981) ZiF Forschungsgruppe 1981–2, Preprint Series, 7.

Hain, P. *et al.* (eds) *Policing the Police*, Vol. II (Calder, 1980).

Haldane, A. R. B., *New Ways Through The Glens* (Nelson, 1962).

Heald, D. A., *Public Expenditure* (Robertson, 1983).

Heclo, H., 'Issue Networks and the Executive Establishment', in King, A. (ed.) *The New American Political System* (American Enterprise Institute, 1978) pp. 87–124.

Heirs, B. and Pehrson, G., *The Mind of the Organization*, 2nd edn (Harper & Row, 1982).

Heller, J., *Catch-22* (Corgi, 1969) (First pub'd 1962).

Herman, R. D. (ed.) *Gambling* (Harper & Row, 1967).

Hodgkinson, C., *Towards a Philosophy of Administration* (Blackwell, 1978).

Hodgson, G., *All Things to All Men: The False Promise of The Modern American Presidency* (Weidenfeld & Nicolson, 1980).

Hogwood, B. W., 'Analyzing Industrial Policy: A Multi-Perspective Approach', *Public Administration Bulletin*, 29 (April 1979) pp. 18–42.

Hood, C. C., *The Limits of Administration* (Wiley, 1976).

Hood, C. C. and Dunsire, A., *Bureaumetrics* (Gower, 1981).

Hood, C. C. and Wright, M. (eds) *Big Government in Hard Times* (Robertson, 1981).

Jarvie, I. C., *Towards a Sociology of the Cinema: A Comparative Essay on the Structure and Functioning of a Major Entertainment Industry* (Routledge & Kegan Paul, 1970).

Kagan, R. A., *Regulatory Justice: Implementing a Wage–Price Freeze* (Russell Sage Foundation, 1978).

Kast, F. E. and Rosenzweig, J. E., *Contingency Views of Organization and Management* (Science Research Associates, 1973).

Kaufmann, F.-X., 'Social Policy and Social Services', in Grunow, D. and Hegner, F. (eds) *Welfare or Bureaucracy? Problems of Matching Social Services to Clients' Needs* (Oelgeschlager, Gunn & Hain, 1980) pp. 29–43.

Kaufman, F.-X. and Rosewitz, B., 'Typisierung und Klassifikation politischer Maßnahmen' (mimeo, ZiF, Universität Bielefeld, 1982).

King, A., 'Overload: Problems of Governing in the 1970s', *Political Studies*, XXIII (1975) pp. 162–74.

Klaus, G., *Kybernetik und Gesellschaft*, 3rd edn (Deutscher Verlag der Wissenschaften, 1973).

Knightley, P., *First Casualty: From the Crimea to Vietnam: War Correspondent as Hero, Propagandist and Mythmaker* (Deutsch, 1975).

Knoepfel, P. and Wiedner, H., 'Normbildung und Implementation: Interessenberücksichtigungsmuster in Programmstrukturen von Luftreinhaltepolitiken', in Mayntz, R. (ed.) *Implementation Politischer Programme* (Hain, 1980) pp. 82–104.

Kogan, M., *The Politics of Education: E. Boyle and A. Crosland in Conversation with M. Kogan* (Penguin, 1971).

Kohlmeier, L. M., *The Regulators: Watchdog Agencies and the Public Interest* (Harper & Row, 1969).

Kramer, N. J. T. A. and Smit, J. de, *Systems Thinking: Concepts and Notions* (Martinus Nijhoff, 1977).

Larsen, E., *Wit as a Weapon: The Political Joke in History* (Muller, 1980).

Lasswell, H. D. and Kaplan, A., *Power and Society: A Framework for Political Inquiry* (Yale University Press, 1950).

Lasswell, H. D., Lerner, D. and Speier, H. (eds) *Propaganda and Communication in World History* (Hawaii University Press, 1980).

Lasswell, H. D. and Fox, M. B., *The Signature of Power: Buildings, Communication and Policy* (Transaction, 1979).

Llewellyn Smith, Sir H., *The Board of Trade* (Putnams, 1928).

Lowi, T. J., 'American Business, Public Policy, Case Studies and Political Theory', *World Politics*, XVI, 2 (1964), pp. 677–715.

Lowi, T. J., *The End of Liberalism* (Norton, 1969).

Lowi, T. J. and Stone, A. (eds) *Nationalizing Government: Public Policies in America* (Sage, 1978).

Lyman, S. M. and Scott, M. B., *The Drama of Social Reality* (Oxford University Press, 1975).

Lynn, J. and Jay, A. (eds) *Yes Minister: The Diaries of a Cabinet Minister*, Vol. I (British Broadcasting Corporation, 1981).

Machin, H., *The Prefect in French Public Administration* (Croom Helm, 1977).

Madgwick, D. and Smythe, T., *The Invasion of Privacy* (Pitman, 1974).

Martin, R. M., *Trades Union Congress: The Growth of a Pressure Group 1868–1976* (Oxford University Press, 1980).

Marx, K. and Engels, F., *L'Idéologie Allemande* (First pubd 1932), ed. Badia, G. (Editions Sociales, 1968).

Mayntz, R., 'Die Implementation politischer Programme: Theoretische Uberlegungen zu einem neuen Forschungsgebiel', *Die Verwaltung*, X (1977) pp. 51–66.

Mayntz, R. (ed.) *Implementation Politischer Programme* (Hain, 1980).

Mayntz, R., 'The Changing Conditions of Effective Public Policy: A New Challenge for Policy Analysis' (ZiF, Universität Bielefeld, 1981) ZiF Forschungsgruppe 1981–2, Preprint Series, 9.

Mishan, E. J., 'Comment' (on Buchanan, J. M., 'Public Goods and

Natural Liberty') in Wilson, T. and Skinner, A. S. (eds) *The Market and the State: Essays in Honour of Adam Smith* (Oxford University Press, 1976), pp. 286–91.

Mitchell, J., *Reminiscences of My Life in the Highlands*, Vol. I (David & Charles, 1971) (First pubd 1883).

Mitchison, R., *History of Scotland* (Methuen, 1970).

Nelson, R. and Winter, S., *An Evolutionary Theory of Economic Capabilities and Behaviour* (Harvard University Press, 1982).

Newman, O., *Defensible Space: Crime Prevention Through Urban Design* (Macmillan, 1972).

O'Connor, J., *The Fiscal Crisis of the State* (St. Martin's Press, 1973).

Offe, C., *Berufsbildungsreform: Eine Fallstudie* über Reformpolitik (Suhrkamp, 1975).

Ogilvy-Webb, M., *The Government Explains: A Study of the Information Services* (Allen & Unwin, 1965).

Olmstead, C., 'Analyzing a Pack of Cards', in Herman, R. D. (ed.) *Gambling* (Harper & Row, 1967) pp. 136–52.

Ostrom, V., 'Who Guides, Controls and Evaluates Whose Performance: An Inquiry into Some Basic Constitutional Considerations', paper presented to conference on 'Analyzing Interactions among Multiple Actors in the Public Sector', ZiF, Universität Bielefeld, 1–6 July 1982.

Peters, B. G. and Hogwood, B. W., 'Policy Succession: The Dynamics of Policy Change', *Studies in Public Policy*, 69 (University of Strathclyde Centre for the Study of Public Policy, 1980).

Ranney, A. (ed.) *Political Science and Public Policy* (Markham, 1968).

Richardson, J. J. and Jordan, A. G., *Governing Under Pressure* (Robertson, 1979).

Rogaly, J., *Grunwick* (Penguin, 1977).

Rollo, J., 'The Special Patrol Group', in Hain, P. *et al.* (eds) *Policing the Police*, Vol. II (Calder, 1980).

Rose, R., 'On the Priorities of Government: A Developmental Analysis of Public Policies', *European Journal of Political Research*, IV, 3 (1976) pp. 247–89.

Rose, R., 'What if Anything is Wrong with Big Government?' *Studies in Public Policy*, 76 (University of Strathclyde Centre for the Study of Public Policy, 1981).

Rose, R. and Peters, B. G., *Can Government Go Bankrupt*? (Basic Books, 1978).

Rosenberg, W. G. and Young, M. B., *Transforming Russia and China: Revolutionary Struggle in the Twentieth Century* (Oxford University Press, 1982).

Rowat, D. C. (ed.) *Administrative Secrecy in Developed Countries* (Columbia University Press, 1979).

Sabine, B. E. V., *A History of Income Tax* (Allen & Unwin, 1966).

Salisbury, R., 'The Analysis of Public Policy: A Search for Themes and Roles', in Ranney, A. (ed.) *Political Science and Public Policy* (Markham, 1968) pp. 151–75.

Schaffer, B. and Lamb, G., *Can Equity Be Organized?* (Gower, 1981).

Scharpf, F. W., 'Die Rolle des Staates im westlichen Wirtschaftssystem: zwischen Krise und Neuorientierung', in Weizsäcker, C. C. von (ed.) *Staat und Wirtschaft: Verhandlungen auf der Arbeitstagung des Vereins für Sozialpolitik, Hamburg 1978*, Schriften Neue Folge/ Verein für Sozialpolitik, 102 (Duncker & Humblot, 1979).

Self, P. and Storing, H. J., *The State and the Farmer* (Allen & Unwin, 1962).

Sennett, R., *The Fall of Public Man* (Cambridge University Press, 1977).

Simon, H. A., Smithburg, D. W. and Thompson, V. A., *Public Administration* (Knopf, 1950).

Smith, A., *The Wealth of Nations*, 2 vols (Dent, 1910) (First pubd 1776).

Steel, T., *The Life and Death of St. Kilda* (Fontana, 1975).

Stockwell, J., *In Search of Enemies: A CIA Story* (Norton, 1978).

Stone, C. D., *Where The Law Ends: The Social Control of Corporate Behavior* (Harper & Row, 1975).

Taxation, LXXIV, 1935 (7 November 1964).

Thomson, A. W. J. and Engleman, S. R., *The Industrial Relations Act* (Robertson, 1975).

Troup, Sir E., *The Home Office* (Putnam, 1925).

Underwood, R. (ed.) *The Future of Scotland* (Croom Helm, 1977).

Weidenbaum, M. L., *The Modern Public Sector: New Ways of Doing the Government's Business* (Basic Books, 1969).

Weiss, C. H. and Barton, A. H. (eds) *Making Bureaucracies Work* (Sage, 1980).

Wigham, E. L., *Strikes and the Government 1893–1974* (Macmillan, 1976).

Wildavsky, A., *The Art and Craft of Policy Analysis: Speaking Truth to Power* (Macmillan, 1980).

Wilson, T. and Skinner, A. S. (eds), *The Market and the State: Essays in Honour of Adam Smith* (Oxford University Press, 1976).

Winnifrith, Sir J., *Ministry of Agriculture, Fisheries and Food* (Allen & Unwin, 1962).

Wittfogel, K. A., *Oriental Despotism: A Comparative Study of Total Power* (Yale University Press, 1959).

Wrong, D. H., *Power: Its Forms, Bases and Uses* (Blackwell, 1979).

Zijderveld, A. C., *On Clichés: The Supersedure of Meaning by Function in Modernity* (Routledge & Kegan Paul, 1979).

Index

7 Government as a Tool-Kit

Suppose, for example, as the French mathematician Henri Poincaré reminded us, that instead of a finite number of chemical elements there were billions of them; that some were not common and others rare, but they were uniformly distributed so that every time we picked up a new pebble, there would be a great probability of its being formed of some unknown substance. If that were so, all that we know of other pebbles would be worthless. Before each object we would be as a newborn babe.

(Heirs and Pehrson, 1982, p. 29)

Thinking of government as a tool-kit helps us to do at least three things. First, it can help us to make sense of the apparent complexity of government activity as some combination of a relatively limited basic range of instruments, we have what cyberneticians call a 'variety reducer', or, in plain language, a mode of simplification. The 'table of elements' that is referred to in the epigraph above is precisely such a variety reducer, enabling us to make sense of a chemical world that would otherwise be intelligible only by laborious verbal description.

Second, and conversely, the 'tool-kit' approach can serve as a variety generator. It can help us to 'think laterally', to identify and generate alternative possible ways in which government might go about tackling a job.

Third, the approach can provide us with a yardstick for comparison. We can compare governments, agencies, policy fields in terms of the range and mix of tools that they employ. We can trace how the instruments used by government to tackle some problem or other may change over time.

These themes were sketched out in Chapter 1. What this chapter does is to develop them a little, in the order that they were set out above. The aim is to show some of the applications of the style of thinking set out in Parts I and II.

Making sense of complexity

Government administration is so complex that we have to find ways of making it simple. Look at it one way, as we saw in Chapter 1, and the variety of operations and activities seems fantastic, defying comprehension by any single mind. But in another sense all government activities can be understood as different mixes and combinations of a relatively small number of generic administrative tools, many of them ancient in origin.

The idea of government administration as the generation of endless permutations of a limited set of standard routines, or variations on a few basic themes, has parallels with the economist's use of three or four basic 'factors of production' to describe any production function that exists or might exist. When a new 'problem' or policy comes along, government does not, typically, invent an entirely new implement for putting its purpose into effect. How could it? Government (whatever it might like us to think) is not peopled by super-intelligent beings. Geniuses who are capable of generating qualitative novelty are as few and far between in government as anywhere else. Mostly, government must work with the implements that it already has, adapting them to a new context as best it can. (This can happen for reasons other than sheer lack of invention, of course, often government can economise on bureaucracy by using already existing instruments, relying on what currently exists 'on the ground'.)

It could not be otherwise. Complexity in nature – and in artifice – is invariably built on the architectonics of producing high variety from a relatively small number of basic units. There is no other model. Music, dancing, language are cases of enormous complexity generated from a quite limited set of routines, the very limited number of morphemes that we use in speech. Equally, each individual item, though unique in itself, can readily be identified as a permutation of some or all of these routines, even by someone who has never seen or heard it before.

In fact, even when we cut down the variety-producing potential of combinatorially productive mechanisms (like music or language) to the tiniest fraction of what they are capable of producing, we are *still* left with very high variety. In everyday conversation and 'shop talk', for example, we use nothing like the full potential of our language. We speak in clichés, unthinkingly stringing together hackneyed words and stale phrases. Yet it is possible to communicate quite efficiently by speaking

Chapter 9 concludes the book with two themes. First, it considers ways in which the overall balance among government's instruments might change over time, and looks at the kind of evidence that might indicate how that balance has shifted in the recent past. Second, it looks at the question of whether there are limitations to government's tool-box and whether there are circumstances in which its tools will *not* serve.

III ANALYSING GOVERNMENT'S TOOLS IN USE

Looking at the instruments that have been described in the last four chapters is one possible way of answering Richard Rose's 'plain man's question' about what government does – rather differently from the way that he himself answered it (Rose, 1976).

In principle we might collect examples of government's applying its instruments merely for the pleasure of coming across new varieties, just as we might collect stamps or railway engine numbers for their own sake, and require no more justification than that.

What this part of the book aims to do, however, is to step back again from the eight basic tools outlined in Chapter 1 and elaborated in Parts I and II and to look at them as a whole. We move from the stamp-collecting stage to a different kind of analysis. In fact, we now return to the reasons set out in Chapter 1 for making it worthwhile to explore government's tools.

Chapter 7 takes up that theme again and discusses some of the applications that can arise from thinking of government activities as the operation of a set of tools. We can 'read' government actions in a different way; we can be alerted to alternative possibilities; we can make comparisons and trace out changes over time.

Chapter 8 then goes on to a slightly different tack. It explores how government might go about picking tools for any given job. Must such a choice always be a shot in the dark? Are there clear-cut ways of distinguishing good from bad applications?

detection mix employed by government is also likely to be influenced by a third broad element, namely the state of government's wider social and political environment. The more recalcitrant the quarry, the more active the search will have to be if government is to be effective. On a larger scale we can suppose that the more government is disliked, feared or distrusted, the wider will be the area over which subjects perceive their interests to diverge from those of government and the deeper the divergence will be.

Thus the less well disposed the public at large are to a political regime, the more government detection will have to be conducted by active rather than by passive means and by modes other than voluntary ones. Subjects will be less disposed to inform government unless they are legally required to do so or unless they can see a direct benefit from so doing. The flow of voluntary information may thus be reduced. At a higher level of disaffection, the rewards offered by government as a means of drawing in information, will be left unclaimed; or higher rewards may be needed to achieve the same effect. Passive obligation-to-notify and return systems may be ignored, evaded or openly flouted, as in the case of the British suffragettes' refusal to co-operate in the 1911 census.

In these circumstances government may find itself turning increasingly to interrogations, inspections, propositions and involuntary detection by hidden scanners. For example, the British government in the 'low consensus' context of Northern Ireland has found itself laboriously conducting house-to-house searches to collect information about colour of front door, type of heating system and type of furniture for about half the houses in the province, in order to be able to check the identity of suspects more easily (Campbell in Hain, 1980, p. 109).

Such a change in the active–passive balance of the detection tools discussed here will in turn inevitably tend to make government more expensive and bureaucracy-intensive per unit of information obtained, for reasons which have already been explained. A government in this position has a hard choice to make. The choice may lie between accepting a reduction in the intake of useful information (possibly rendering government less effective in consequence), or trying to increase fiscal exactions – themselves in large part dependent on the quality of information intake – to support a more active information-gathering stance. To adopt either of these choices runs the risk of involving government in a vicious circle, in the form of a spiral either of declining effectiveness and reduced information intake, or of rising disaffection and of increasing government demands for compulsory information.

Indeed, when the social context is one of disaffection, government may well *deliberately* want to shut down some of its detectors, for reasons discussed in Chapter 2. If the news is all bad news, government may not want to listen; and, as we have already observed, embarrassing information that is not collected does not have to be kept secret. But this is, of course, a slippery slope. A government without detectors cannot govern at all.